David A. MacLennan

PREACHING WEEK BY WEEK

Ideas

Insights

Illustrations

FLEMING H. REVELL COMPANY

Preface

Preaching Week By Week is the privilege and obligation
of Christ's preachers. To some harassed pastors the weekly
sermon may seem to be the penalty of their vocation. Life, for
ministers in Canada and the United States, is "so daily." It
is also weekly—in terms of the sermon or sermons which
must be prepared once every seven days.

True, the ultimate source of our words is the living Word
which comes to us through the written Word of scripture.
"How is it," asked a famous preacher's hearer, "that he always has something new and good to say?" "Because," was
the answer, "he lives so near to God that God tells him
things that He does not tell other people." Nevertheless, even
the preacher who does not let the organization man in him
limit his communion with God needs ideas, insights, illustrations.

This book has been prepared for the busy pastor. I hope
sincerely that it contains some usable aids. Some of it appeared in different form in my articles in *Church Manage-
ment* magazine. All of it is now offered my brother preachers in the hope that they may find sermon starters for their
own preaching week by week.

DAVID A. MAC LENNAN

Rochester, New York

Contents

II CHRISTIAN CONVICTIONS

III CHRISTIAN ANTIDOTE FOR CRISIS

IV CHRISTIAN CALENDAR

I

CHRISTIAN LIVING

1

Mastering Inferiority Feelings

... SO I WAS AFRAID, AND I WENT AND HID YOUR TAL-
ENT IN THE GROUND. HERE YOU HAVE WHAT IS YOURS
—MATTHEW 25:25, RSV.

Who doesn't know what it is to feel inadequate and inferior? Most of us explain our defeats in terms of what we probably mislabel our "inferiority complexes." Faced with a personal problem or task, we act as if our feelings of inferiority and the job were too much. Scientists, military leaders and government spokesmen may be perplexed by problems of outer space; we are depressed by problems of inner space and a lack of interior resources. To this need, Christ and the Christian faith bring the answer.

I. Christ painted a picture of a man who felt basically inferior. A wealthy employer gives members of his staff certain sums of money to invest as best they can. Not everyone receives the same amount. Some get more and some get less, but all receive something. This emphasizes the truth of the gospel that every person has something to contribute to the total scheme of life.

One talent may not seem to be worth much today, but in Jesus' time a talent was equal to several hundreds of our dollars. In the parable, the man entrusted with this considerable amount sits down and compares his one talent with the larger number more fortunate persons have been given. Comparison creates a feeling of deprivation, and he begins to talk to himself about what he cannot do because of insufficient capital.

Envy may be a factor in feelings of inferiority. It may induce self-disparagement, self-contempt, and a sort of spiritual paralysis. Then rationalization takes over: "It's absurd to expect me to do anything with this trifling amount. If I had ten times as much, I could really produce something, but not with this measly talent! I'll bury it and keep it safe. I'll not do any harm. I'll do nothing."

II. But the day of accounting comes. Instead of appreciation for his carefulness and prudence, he hears the master say, "You wicked and slothful servant!" The question is not "Have you played it safe?" but "What have you done with what life you have been given?"

III. What is Christ's cure for feelings of inferiority? (A) Face the fact that apart from God in Christ, every man is inadequate and unworthy. As a psychiatrist said to a patient: "Let's face it. You don't have an inferiority complex. You *are* inferior!" The divine Physician could speak similarly to every man and every woman. But God never lets any of His children remain inferior if He can help them. And He is able to help even the most beaten among us. (B) Having faced the feelings, and perhaps uncovered some of the reasons for them, take Christ with you to fight and overcome your enemy. Be yourself, not the many-talented, "superior" person. But be yourself at your best, in Christ and for His cause. Go in the strength of God's almighty Son by telling Him your need and claiming His help. You can find power through prayer, commitment and companionship with the unseen Lord. You will find yourself, with Christ, "able for anything" (Philippians 4:13, MOFFATT).

2

When You Feel Insecure

> ...LET US BE GRATEFUL FOR RECEIVING A KINGDOM
> THAT CANNOT BE SHAKEN, AND THUS LET US OFFER TO
> GOD ACCEPTABLE WORSHIP ... —HEBREWS 12:28, RSV.

Psychology and psychotherapy provide much help for those who must live with or overcome feelings of insecurity, but Christ's gospel provides the sovereign cure.

I. Christ's mind in us enables us to recognize that the search for security is characteristic of living creatures, and that it is a primary need implanted by the Creator.

II. Christian maturity also requires us to recognize that insecurity is normal in this dynamic world our Father has provided for us.

III. Christianity teaches that worldly security is not the highest good.

IV. Yet Christ offers true security in the midst of much that is insecure. Membership in His Kingdom alone is stability, and to be within this society through our trust and obedience to the divine King is to be related to the absolute and final order.

3

Winning the Battle of Loneliness

AND WHEN JESUS CAME TO THE PLACE, HE LOOKED UP AND SAID TO HIM, "ZACCHAEUS, MAKE HASTE AND COME DOWN; FOR I MUST STAY AT YOUR HOUSE TODAY." SO HE MADE HASTE AND CAME DOWN, AND RECEIVED HIM JOYFULLY—LUKE 19:5-6, RSV.

... YET I AM NOT ALONE, FOR THE FATHER IS WITH ME—JOHN 16:32, RSV.

An Old Testament story describes how the walls of Jericho came tumbling down under the shouts of Joshua's troops. In a New Testament story, walls built around the personality of a man from Jericho dissolve under the gracious treatment of Jesus. The Jericho man was Zacchaeus, a lonely man. Doubtless, his conduct accounted for his isolation from his fellow men. A collaborator with the enemy, a grafter, a greedy and selfish character, he would be an unpopular citizen in any town. Zacchaeus was also unusually short of stature, and inferiority feelings breed easily in such a person. He ached with loneliness.

Ours is not only the age of anxiety, publicity and atomic fission; it is also an age of chilling loneliness. Strategy for winning the crucial battle against loneliness and rejection may be learned from the encounter of Jesus with Jericho's lonely man.

I. Jesus asked Zacchaeus to "come off his perch." Jesus knew loneliness, although He has more friends today than any other person. Repeatedly, in crises—wilderness temptations, the transfiguration, Gethsemane—He was alone. Yet He showed no trace of self-pity. Christ helps us to accept a certain amount of loneliness as part of the price of being human and being made in God's spiritual likeness. We may be joined in one family of mankind but, like islands joined together underneath the estranging sea, our separation is often deep. Jesus also taught, and teaches, that we are made for friendship, to love and be loved. We are unnecessarily lonely because we try to live contrary to God's plan. Loneliness is more a matter of insulation than isolation.

II. Jesus asked Zacchaeus to exercise faith. Zacchaeus was short, not only in stature, but in confidence in others, and trust builds personal relationships. Take the risk, Jesus seems to say, even if people have let you down. There are great persons in whom you can believe. Believe in the supreme Person.

III. Engage in adventures of friendship. Either as the result of the impact of Jesus' personality, or the result of an interview unreported in our brief gospel account, Zacchaeus tried—to use Dr. Albert Schweitzer's phrase—"investing in humanity." "In a needy world like ours," said Arthur Pearson, a famous benefactor of the sightless, and himself physically blind, "anybody can have friendship who will give it." Why not try matching experiences with another? Paul was willing to become a Greek, a slave, anything, to win another to a full life. "Am I my brother's keeper?" Perhaps not, but you are your brother's brother—in Christ.

IV. The sovereign weapon for vanquishing loneliness is friendship with Christ. He admits us to His friendship, but we must admit Him to ours. When we want Him, He comes; and we never are alone.

4

How to Be Adequate in Spite of Everything

SCRIPTURE LESSON—MARK 6, RSV.

I. Christ meets our need when we have too much to do. "... many were coming and going, and they had no leisure even to eat" (Mark 6:31, RSV). Crowded hours and busy days can be exhilarating, but with the excitement comes danger, too. We can become extreme activists and can almost believe that *doing* is more important than *being*. Quiet, prayer, worship, meditation—centering down in God's Spirit—are resources we need. We must follow Jesus' direction: "Come away by yourselves to a lonely place, and rest a while" (Mark 6:31, RSV).

II. Christ has the answer when evil appears to be winning. Jesus was deeply grieved when He learned that John the Baptist had been imprisoned and killed, but He saw John's martyrdom within the larger pattern of God's purposes.

III. Christ helps us to meet the so-called "atheistic facts" of human pain and undeserved suffering. Note in this chapter the references to Jesus' contacts with sick persons. Jesus believed it to be God's will that sickness should be healed, and He not only proceeded to heal the sick but also transmitted to His disciples His power to heal. What we must bring to pain is unwavering trust in God and in God's power to use fallible human agents— ourselves and our fellow Christians—as instruments of His healing power.

5

You, Too, Can Learn to Love

LET YOUR LOVE BE A REAL THING . . .—ROMANS 12:9, MOFFATT.

. . . LET US CONSIDER HOW TO STIR UP ONE ANOTHER TO LOVE AND GOOD DEEDS—HEBREWS 10:24, MOFFATT.

The suggestion for this message comes from Melvin E. Wheatley, whose sermon "You Can Learn to Love" begins with the proposition that nothing else in life matters except to be loved and to love.

I. Love is available. Any person, with divine help, can learn to love and be lovable. God made us for love, but for most of us it is a formidable task. Edwin Holt Hughes used to say that one of two facts applies to any preacher who preaches that it is easy to love one's neighbor: "Either he has never tried it, or he has awfully good neighbors!" Is it easy to love individuals? And is it easy to love your self genuinely?

II. "Real love is an affirmative relationship that can be learned through positive experience that can be shared." So writes Dr. Wheatley. When persons fail in love it may be due to a failure to experience a loving relationship. How do we learn to have positive experiences? (A) We must be willing to love a little before we can love a lot. Before we can love enemies we must learn to remember our friends, to love them in the New Testament sense of desiring to bring our their best. Recall Jesus' teaching about a failure in a love-relationship with a brother: "Leave there thy gift before the altar . . ." (Matthew 5:24, kjv), and go and learn how to live in harmony and affection with those estranged from you. Relate yourself affirmatively to a difficult neighbor before you worship the God whom you have not seen. (B) Learn to love from those who have mastered this essential art. Have we not learned to love because we have been loved by a parent? As Leon Saul says, the answer to the familiar quip, "What is the best thing a father can do for his children?" is "Love mother."

Men and women in Jesus' company learned to love from His love. They became more compassionate because they saw His compassion for the rejected, the lost, the unlovable. Jesus treated them as potentially loving, lovable souls. Indeed, with drabs from the streets and alleyways, as well as with greedy and corrupt tax collectors and shifty citizens, He loved them into newness of life. Within a few years, pagan observers of the behavior of the Master's disciples admiringly, and with no trace of sarcasm, exclaimed, "See how these Christians love one another!"

To be of maximum helpfulness, a preacher should spell out ways of learning to love in the school of Christ and in the immediacies of our own living.

Where Are You?

WHERE ARE YOU?—GENESIS 3:9, RSV.

On life's voyage, meaning and significance come when we know where we are.

I. Where are you in relation to time? Do you experience the eternal in the midst of time?

II. Where are you in relation to life's great movements of thought and action? Are you stuck fast in yesterday? Is reminiscence or reverie replacing reveille?

III. Where are you in relation to life's deep, durable satisfactions?

IV. Where are you in relation to the supreme Reality? Are you a spiritual vagrant? Are you an exile or a displaced person in a universe which is one of our heavenly Father's many rooms?

How Big Is One?

ANOTHER OF HIS DISCIPLES, ANDREW, SIMON PETER'S BROTHER, SAID TO HIM, THERE IS A LITTLE BOY HERE, WHO HAS [WITH HIM] FIVE BARLEY LOAVES AND TWO SMALL FISH; BUT WHAT ARE THEY AMONG SO MANY PEOPLE?—JOHN 6:8-9, AMPLIFIED.

I. "How big is one?" This question of Edward Weeks, editor of the *Atlantic Monthly,* must be considered by every civilized person and certainly every Christian. In the face of global problems and titanic questions, how important is one person? Mr. Weeks is right in saying that the American concept of bigness has affected our private lives and thinking:

> We have been in love with bigness ever since the adolescence of our democracy. . . . Our first hero of the frontier was a super-man, Davy Crockett, who could outshoot, outfight, and outwoo anyone.[1]

Our worship of bigness has done some questionable things to us as persons. Mergers, huge corporations, supermarkets and news-paper chains make individual enterprise and individual taste difficult. We enjoy the benefits of mass production but we are uneasy and even rebellious when "consolidations grow to the size of a giant octopus." Huge aggregations of power exert pressures that are difficult to resist. What can one person do to improve conditions? How much can an individual accomplish for honesty and peace, or in feeding the other half of the world's population who go to bed hungry every night?

II. God declares that one person is more important and more valuable than systems, corporations or cartels, which so frequently ignore, minimize or ruthlessly trample individuals. Christ's action in feeding the hungry thousands is a picture of the divine attitude toward "little people," toward the one among many. He used the small boy's small contribution. In His teaching Jesus always stressed the importance of the individual. No man is an island, and apart from others we cannot realize our utmost. Community is God's will. Private religion is not the religion of the Bible. But one lost sheep, one lost coin or one lost boy justifies any sacrifice necessary to find and restore. "God so loved the world"—a world of persons.

III. Accept Christ's evaluation of yourself and dedicate it to Him and to the service of your fellow souls, and you will know the answer to the question, "How big is one?" Edward Weeks speaks with Christian insight when he says that "in an atomic age self-reliance and self-restraint are needed as they have never been before." Weakened by self-distrust and mutual suspicion, we must have persons who will "stand forth, upright and ready to speak the hard truth for the public good," for "one is as big as you yourself can make it."

How Independent Should We Be?

> ... BOUND IN THE BUNDLE OF THE LIVING ... .—I SAM-
> UEL 25:29, RSV.

Robert Burns praised "the glorious privilege of being independent." But—

I. Are we wise when we are too independent to take advice?

II. Do we ever become adequate for life before we admit that we cannot cope with life by ourselves?

III. Should we not acknowledge, with St. Paul, the anonymous creditors we have?

IV. Does not the railroad ticket speak of our predicament: "Worthless if detached"?

Finding Genuine Happiness

> I CAME THAT THEY MAY HAVE LIFE, AND HAVE IT ABUN-
> DANTLY—JOHN 10:10, RSV.

At the end of a biography about a writer of mystery stories are these words:

> Edgar Wallace had been avid for life. He had begun with nothing, and now he had everything that he had consciously demanded. Money, fame, power—they were all his. The only

thing which in these last years had somehow failed him was personal happiness.[2]

How valuable are money, fame or power if a man is unhappy inside himself? Robert Louis Stevenson insisted that every person had a duty to be happy and that a happy man is "a radiating focus of good will" and his entrance into a room is as though another candle were lighted.

How can we find happiness and still retain a profound faith and way of living? Here are three elements in a formula which has been learned in the school of Christ and tested by countless persons across nineteen centuries:

I. Keep your conscience unafraid. Consider Job's resolution: ". . . my heart shall not reproach me so long as I live" (27:6, KJV).

II. Invest yourself in a cause that is significant enough to take you out of yourself. Jesus challenged us to lose our lives for His sake and thereby to find real life.

III. Cultivate what G. T. Bellhouse calls "that good sense of *nowness*." William Osler said we should live each day in day-tight compartments. One day at a time holds sufficient joy and sufficient evil to satisfy any valiant soul.

IV. Keep yourself in the love of God by dwelling deep in the "love divine, all loves excelling."[3]

10

How to Be Happy Though Religious

MAY THE GOD OF HOPE FILL YOU WITH ALL JOY . . .—
ROMANS 15:13, RSV.

Everybody who is normal desires happiness, and we spend millions of dollars trying to secure it. The best-seller list of books gives evidences of this ceaseless quest, and trustworthy spiritual guides assure us that God wants us to be happy. Certainly Jesus came to give us the secret of the joy-filled life, and He Himself was a singularly happy Person. How may we enjoy religion as He did?

I. Forget about being happy. The really happy men and women have forgotten about the pursuit of happiness in their complete immersion in a worthy cause, in a noble love and in a giving away of themselves for the sake of another.

II. Stop being religious and start being Christian. Religion is a set of rules, a collection of maxims, a string of guideposts; a matter of imparting information and then seeking to incorporate it by "sweating it out." Christ came to save us from that kind of religion and He offers deliverance by revealed power, love and holiness, which alone bring enduring joy.

III. Joy is an "inside job." Before we can experience Christ's radiant happiness, we must help His Spirit clean up the foul things inside our soul's house. Then we must learn to accept ourselves by surrendering ourselves to the great God who will cleanse, forgive and make us whole.

11

Is Time Getting Shorter?

MAKE THE BEST USE OF YOUR TIME, DESPITE ALL THE DIFFICULTIES OF THESE DAYS. DON'T BE VAGUE BUT FIRMLY GRASP WHAT YOU KNOW TO BE THE WILL OF GOD—EPHESIANS 5:16-17, PHILLIPS.

Is an hour of our time actually as short as a quarter of an hour two hundred years ago? If it is, why do we accomplish so much less than we feel we should? Is it temperament? Is it our frenzied era? Is it because a five-day week induces more indolence? Or has Philip Toynbee made a point in saying it derives from "our frightening lack of certitude" and our questioning of every value of the past? Without deep Christian faith, can a person be productive in an adequate way?

I. Recover your belief that God is, and that His purpose includes everything we call a "spiritual value." He makes Himself known through Jesus Christ. By His Holy Spirit He leads us into the truth that life is sacred and is not to be treated as trivial, and that time is one of God's gifts and is not to be killed. Recreation and loafing may use time profitably. But worship, witnessing for Christ and working for a truly Christian world order are also on our agenda.

II. Budget your time. We are called to a stewardship of our days and years as well as our money and ability. Do we take time to be holy?—to be whole and healthy in an inclusive sense? Do we make time for God and for those in the family and community who need us?

III. Live this day as if it were fresh from the loom of God. If you knew that this was to be your final day, how would you use it? ". . . now is the day of salvation" (II Corinthians 6:2, RSV).

12

Use the Time You Have

ARE THERE NOT TWELVE HOURS IN THE DAY? IF ANY ONE WALKS IN THE DAY, HE DOES NOT STUMBLE, BECAUSE HE SEES THE LIGHT OF THIS WORLD. BUT IF ANY ONE WALKS IN THE NIGHT, HE STUMBLES, BECAUSE THE LIGHT IS NOT IN HIM—JOHN 11:9, RSV.

You have twelve hours every day, says the Master of life. But you must walk—not merely rest, repine, fret and go around in circles. Time fascinates us. Time passes, we say, but the poet was right: "No, we pass, time stays."

No Christian need apologize for loafing. Life is alternation. Toil and rest, work and play, and activity—physical, mental, intellectual and spiritual—characterize the balanced life. Nevertheless most of us need not have many birthdays to realize that "time's awastin'."

Preaching on the topic "What on Earth Are You Doing With Your Time?" Melvin E. Wheatley said that the people who do things well are not those who have more time than the rest of us; they are persons who have "firmer hands on their time." He offered these suggestions:

I. *Discriminate* in your use of time. Determine your priorities. Life is like a theater or an auditorium that has only so many seats. With these occupied by varied interests and activities, there are no more seats for others. Jesus had to be engaged in His Father's business.

II. *Alternate* is the second key to Christian use of our time. Richard C. Cabot, in his book *What Men Live By*, says that work, love, play and worship are the four basic ingredients of a well-rounded, developing personality.

III. *Concentrate* is the third rule for making the most of our minutes, hours, days and years. "Now hear this," life says to us repeatedly. Do we listen? Do we pay attention? Moments are magical when they are focused on something worth doing, thinking about and praying about.

I would add the following to Dr. Wheatley's outline:

IV. *Dedicate* your time, whether it be much or little, to God. We may have moved on from John Milton's Puritan emphasis on living each minute "As ever in my great Taskmaster's eye,"[4] but we need to offer to God not only our abilities, our money and our energies, which He has entrusted to us, but also our time. To dedicate our days to God is to invest them with eternal worth, and to find them being filled with worthwhile distance run. Think of the ways in which moments and hours can be made to flow in ceaseless praise of One who is both Ancient of Days and eternal Love.

Now I Get Me Up to Wake

NOW PETER AND HIS COMPANIONS HAD BEEN OVER-
POWERED WITH SLEEP, BUT ON WAKING THEY SAW HIS
GLORY . . .—LUKE 9:32, MOFFATT.

Of course you've guessed it! The title is a line from a morning
prayer which someone wrote to complement the familiar "Now
I lay me down to sleep."

> Now I get me up to wake,
> I pray the Lord my soul to shake.

Jesus was about to begin His journey to crucifixion outside
Jerusalem's gate, and He sought God's approval for the step He
was about to take. One sentence in Luke's report of this summit
conference is arresting: "Now Peter and his companions had been
overpowered with sleep, but on waking they saw his glory. . . ."
I. How much do we miss because our minds are asleep? Every
town and city contains respectable residents who are moral and
spiritual somnambulists. They can be more subversive of spiritual
vitality than some other "ists." Our complacent, proud, fellow
citizens sleep on, performing normal actions as if they were wide-
awake. What causes them—and us—to grow somnolent? (A) The
love of comfortableness produces inertia. Whenever any soul is
"at ease in Zion," whether this be a church or a suburb, one cause
may be heavy doses of the drug "tranquillity-at-any-price." (B)
Another cause is unwillingness to think. Mental laziness dopes us.
We may not even care about facing significant questions or our
doubts. We bat back and forth our platitudes, stereotypes and
clichés. (C) Prejudice is soporific. It not only goads men to do
terrifying and nightmarish deeds, but it keeps us unaware of truth.
II. But life comes like a call from a central switchboard in a
hotel, saying, "Time to get up!" (A) Sorrow stirs our sleeping
souls to wakefulness. Tears can cleanse our eyes and make us
perceptive. Have you not observed a person who has grown in

awareness of life's deeper meaning, of human need which can be met, and in understanding of self and of other selves, after he has walked a dark mile with pain or bereavement? More than one critic has said of an artist, "She will be great when she has suffered a little more." Cruel as it seems, the remark carries insight. (B) William Barclay has written that love is a great awakener. He recalls that Robert Browning described two people who fell in love:

> He looked at her as a lover can,
> She looked at him as one who awakes. . . .[5]

What of our love for Christ who first loved us? Many a sacrifice is made and unmentioned by the person making it, not so much for love of humanity as for the love of Him who loved us and gave Himself for us. (C) Thinking about the world mission of Christ's people can "stab . . . [us] broad awake."[6] Children suffering from undernourishment and disease, from cruelty and neglect—whether in Africa, Asia, America or Europe—are little children suffering. What of our own need for forgiveness, for acceptance, and for One whom we can trust and follow?

14

Growing

... GROW IN THE GRACE AND KNOWLEDGE OF OUR LORD AND SAVIOR JESUS CHRIST—II PETER 3:18, RSV.

I. Are we growing in our understanding of others?

II. Are we growing in our knowledge of what really matters in this complex world?

III. Are we growing in our knowledge and love of God?

How to Keep Young in Heart

SCRIPTURE LESSON—JOSHUA 14:6-13, KJV.

When a person eighty-five years old asks for the toughest kind of assignment we are bound to say he is young in heart. That is what Caleb asked for, and that is the kind of person Caleb proved himself to be. When the promised land was being divided, he asked not for lush meadowland. He said to Joshua, ". . . give me this mountain. . . ." The Revised Standard Version translates it: "So now give me this hill country. . . ." The preacher may refer to youthful-spirited persons of our own time, such as Konrad Adenauer and Albert Schweitzer—blooming "octogeraniums," as one eighty-year-old said in an inspired error. At this point also you might define what is meant by "young in heart": One who is eager for new adventures; who, while grateful for the past, lives for today and tomorrow; who, as one has written, shows "a predominance of courage over timidity, of the spirit of adventure over the love of ease."

What are some of the secrets of keeping young in heart?

I. Keep growing old "growingly." An excellent illustration is found in E. Stanley Jones' little devotional manual *Christian Maturity*.[7] The author tells of "Mother Stephens' Day," observed in Santa Monica, California, since 1936.

If we despair of attaining creative living in our nineties we need to be reminded that we are not only as old as our arteries, but as old as our attitudes. When Frank Lloyd Wright, at eighty-three, was asked which of his works he would select as his masterpiece, he answered, "My next one." To stand still is to go into reverse. Recall the Apostle Paul's declaration in II Corinthians 4:16: "So we do not lose heart. Though our outer nature is wasting away, our inner nature is being renewed every day" (RSV).

II. We must live appreciatively. Caleb recalled the day when he brought in the minority report of the scouts sent to spy on Canaan. He recalled with evident gratitude what Moses promised if he would follow God faithfully. Caleb was thankful that although forty-five years had passed since that day, God had kept him alive and the promise was now to be fulfilled. Are we not alive? Despite illnesses, the hazards of traffic, the atom bomb, the cold war? Are we not glad and grateful? We may not have as many birthdays as Caleb, but we are alive. With Rupert Brooke we should say:

> Now God be thanked who has matched us
>   with His hour,
> And caught our youth, and
>   wakened us from sleeping.[8]

Halford Luccock once observed that some Christians seem to have read only a "vinegar Bible"—they seem so sour. I Thessalonians 5:18 gives the directive: "thank God for everything . . ." (MOFFATT).

III. Age does not wither the spirit of the man or woman who asks for worthwhile work, even when the so-called sunset years have begun. Caleb asked, ". . . now give me this hill country. . . ." Don't retire completely, say the experts on aging. Don't quit. Just change your occupation. Too many are old in spirit and temper at the age of thirty, forty, fifty or sixty, because they feel that work is a penance or a punishment imposed by a cruel fate. In London, England, there is the longest moving platform in the world. If you stand on it in Waterloo Station, you and your bags are carried along and up inclines into the Bank of England. Many of us think we would love something like this "Trav-O-Lator" in life, but we were made by God for climbing. Every life needs some climbing places. There is no Christian hymn which says:

> Like the lowly turtle moves the
>   Church of God,
> Brothers, we are dragging where
>   we've always trod.

Caleb chose Hebron, with its rugged, hilly terrain, its enemies and giants. We choose, too often, a garden spot and find it insufferably dull.

IV. Caleb exhibited another characteristic of the young in heart: he had faith in the future. Of course no one can guarantee that we or other members of the human race will have any future. But God is in the tomorrows as He is in the yesterdays and todays. Pessimism is a kind of atheism, and romantic optimism is a kind of unrealistic secular religion. Realistic optimism is born of Christian experience of the great God who has the last word on everything.

V. The great secret of being young in heart and mind is to keep close to the Source of life. No one really grows old in the presence of God. No person ages at the altar of God. When we commit our ways and our lives to the One who is God—over and in and through all, in whom all holds together, who is on every road we take and is Himself the Way—then the years cannot intimidate or depress us. Now and tomorrow we shall live in the grace of God, and by it. There is a wonderful translation of Colossians 2:7 by Dr. J. B. Phillips: "Just as you received Christ, go on living in Him—in simple faith." In doing this, our bodies may grow older, but we shall be youthful in faith, in hope, in love—in Christ.

16

In Orbit

... HE WENT ABOUT DOING GOOD ...—ACTS 10:38, RSV.

When a rocket is in orbit, it is in its rightful course. It has found its true center and it encircles the earth.

I. Jesus our Lord moved from the years of His preparation into His ministry where always He was "in orbit." He was in perfect relationship to the center and soul of every sphere.

II. He encircled the earth, although in His earthly life He never moved much farther than a person moving within the boundaries of an area about the size of our state of Vermont. Yet today He is Lord of the world and Lord of all worlds. In Palestine Jesus encircled and affected for the highest good a world of persons. There was nothing parochial or provincial about His life, His teaching, His death and His resurrection.

III. Are you in orbit? Have you established a relationship to the divine creative Center by which our true life is sustained, empowered and directed? God is life's true Center. By commitment and by trusting our whole self to His love and keeping, we get into orbit. Are you encircling and touching for good the world of persons? How large is your circuit? Does it include the millions you never see but whom you may influence through your intercessory prayers and your support of Christ's world enterprise? Do you shut out any group because of distaste for their color, racial origin, political beliefs or temperamental oddities?

IV. How do we get into orbit? Not by being "fired" with quickly extinguished fuel, but by the enthusiasm we catch from contact with Christ—of whom an apocryphal saying is, "He who is near Me is near the fire"—by maintaining the spiritual glow. Where do we get this fire and how do we maintain this glow? In the upper room of personal devotion, Scripture reading and public worship, and by grappling with the problems of people. And not by just going about, but by going about doing good in the grace and spirit of the Lord Jesus.

17

Don't Neglect These Three R's

> BUT THE LORD WAS WITH JOSEPH AND SHOWED HIM STEADFAST LOVE. . . . AND THE KEEPER OF THE PRISON COMMITTED TO JOSEPH'S CARE ALL THE PRISONERS WHO WERE IN THE PRISON; AND WHATEVER WAS DONE THERE, HE WAS THE DOER OF IT . . .—GENESIS 39:21-22, RSV.

I. *Revelation.* In the light of revelation we realize that we are related to God.

II. *Responsibility.* In the light of our responsibility we must acknowledge our part in our folly and failure, for we—not heredity, environment or other people—are responsible for taking charge of ourselves and turning ourselves over to the One who can remake and redirect us.

III. *Relationships*. In the light of our relationships we know that we are intended for fellowship, for mutual service and for love at its deepest and best.

18

The One for the Road

> THE LORD SHALL PRESERVE THY GOING OUT AND THY
> COMING IN FROM THIS TIME FORTH, AND EVEN FOR
> EVERMORE—PSALM 121:8, KJV.

"Songs for the Road" is a modern definition of the "Songs of Ascent" in the Bible (Revised Standard Version). These spiritual songs were written for travelers, especially for pilgrims who came from all over the ancient world to Jerusalem for the high feasts of the Jewish religion. In the psalmist's day, it was a huge undertaking to go a few hundred miles by land or sea, and a man felt keenly the need for God's protective care. But is our need different, despite the revolution in transportation?

I. Life is a road. Life does not consist of only "thy going out and thy coming in." When we are young, a journey is exciting, even if it is a short trip from one state to another. As we grow older, we are less eager to change location. But what is changeless is the fact of change, and God seems to will that we be mobile: "Get thee out . . ., unto a land that I will shew thee" (Genesis 12:1, KJV).

II. Life in motion, particularly when we have resources to move fairly easily, tends to make us ignore God. Cuthbert R. B. Shapland wrote:

> It is on the thresholds that God is only too often forgotten. . . .
> God is back there, in the old school when prayers are said, and
> in the old church he no longer attends. But he is not in this world
> of business and industry that he is entering.[9]

Think of the millions of individuals in our own nation who have moved several times during the last few years. How easy it is for them to lose touch with God and His people. Transitions are inevitable but we are to take care how we make them. We need divine help and companionship more in the changes of life than in the settled stretches.

III. A poet of long ago assures us that God stands at the boundaries, the frontiers and the thresholds we cross: "There is not where God is not." He was with you in the yesterdays; He is with you today; He will be with you in all the tomorrows, for the tomorrows are His also. In this faith we pray when we say to each other, "Goodbye"—"God be with ye." In some lands across the sea the valedictory is even more pertinent: "Go with God." Has Christ not promised, ". . . lo, I am with you always . . ." (Matthew 28:20, rsv)? "The Lord shall preserve [keep] thy going out and thy coming in . . . for evermore."

19

Buyers' Guide

> WHY DO YOU SPEND YOUR MONEY FOR THAT WHICH IS
> NOT BREAD, AND YOUR LABOR FOR THAT WHICH DOES
> NOT SATISFY?—ISAIAH 55:2, RSV.

Here are some top values listed in God's Buyers' Guide:

I. Life itself. ". . . what shall a man give in return for his life?" (Matthew 16:26, rsv).

II. Love. Without love, life itself is not worth anything.

III. God. We must have God, but we cannot buy God's friendship. The Irish poet William Butler Yeats wrote in his autobiography: "Can you reach God by toil? He gives himself to the pure in heart. He asks nothing but our attention."

Let's Go Back Again

GOD SAID TO JACOB, "ARISE, GO UP TO BETHEL, AND
DWELL THERE; AND MAKE THERE AN ALTAR TO THE GOD
WHO APPEARED TO YOU WHEN YOU FLED FROM YOUR
BROTHER ESAU"—GENESIS 35:1, RSV.

When we consciously or unconsciously strive to return to an age
or condition now forever behind us, psychologists say, in an impressive phrase, that we are indulging in retrogression to the in-
fantile. But here, God is telling Jacob to go back.

I. Jacob had to return to Bethel to recapture the vision which
he had been granted there.

II. To return to our particular Bethel is the secret of advancing.

Get Lost!

... WHOEVER WOULD SAVE HIS LIFE WILL LOSE IT; AND
WHOEVER LOSES HIS LIFE FOR MY SAKE AND THE
GOSPEL'S WILL SAVE IT—MARK 8:35, RSV.

Our proper progenitors would resent and try to ban the slang
directive, "Get lost!" Yet there is wisdom in the idea, for one of
the basic reasons why many of us are miserable is that we cannot
lose ourselves in something greater than ourselves. Logan Pearsall
Smith wrote in his diary: "What a bore it is to wake up every
morning the same person!" He needed to get lost, helpfully. How

can we escape boredom, insignificance and a self-centered existence?

I. Take to the wings of a good book, and particularly the Book.

II. We lose ourselves when we open our eyes to the needs of the world around us.

III. We forget ourselves when we love another person genuinely, seeking not self-fulfillment but rather the fulfillment of the highest possibilities of the one loved.

IV. We are "lost in wonder, love, and praise"[10] when we pray to God and praise Him, not because of what He will do for us, but because of what He has revealed Himself to be.

22

You've Had It!

TRULY, I SAY TO YOU, THEY HAVE THEIR REWARD—
MATTHEW 6:16, RSV.

Here is a slang phrase which I think we owe to World War II servicemen. In those grim days the words usually referred to something bad. When an airman was shot down, his mates said he'd "had it." When a man failed to get a transfer from a hated unit or duty, or if he was charged with an offense, he'd "had it."

In the Scriptures you will find instances of persons, cities and nations having "had it" in this sense. Read what Jesus said of Judas Iscariot in Mark 14:41 (RSV): "It is enough; the hour has come. . . ." The word translated "It is enough" is the same word which was used in signing receipts in the time of Jesus. Literally, it means "he has received." Some scholars suggest that the word referred to Judas, who had just entered the Garden. Was Jesus saying, "He's had it," meaning Judas' payment for the betrayal? The cryptic phrase may have carried something of the meaning of our slang expression.

Thus, when Jesus said that ostentatious or selfish men had received their reward, He was saying that they had been paid in full. They had no further claim on anybody, least of all upon God.

Is there not a Biblical meaning, confirmed in Christian experience, in which we've "had it" in respect to God's deliverance of our lives? Not only should we sing, "I need Thee every hour,"[11] but perhaps, more frequently, "I have Thee every hour."

23

Using the Blots

> I AM HE WHO BLOTS OUT YOUR TRANSGRESSIONS FOR MY OWN SAKE, AND I WILL NOT REMEMBER YOUR SINS —ISAIAH 43:25, RSV.

A young Scottish minister told William Barclay of finding in what Presbyterians call "session records" an interesting report of a man who had been an elder of the kirk many years ago. His name was John Craik. He was an accomplished penman, and was skilled in freehand drawing. When his pupils left blots on their pages, John Craik would use his pen to make a blot the basis for an attractive picture. Invariably he would draw the picture of an angel. Of him it was said, "Surely no man could ever leave a finer memory than the memory that he was the man who produced angels out of blots and turned blots into angels."

I. One of the unequaled achievements of the Christian faith is that it enables God to turn dark, ugly blots of our moral failures and sins into ministering servants of God. Through faith, our very mistakes and defeats can become ministers of grace to renew us and to make us forgiving, as we have been forgiven so much. The words written by Isaiah convey the Word of God: He blots out our transgressions for His own sake, because of His character, His love and His mercy.

II. God, to whom we respond with trust and obedience, gives us resources to find the angel in the dark blot of sorrow. What angel? Acceptance? Yes, but also the angel named Sympathy. A bereaved man wrote to a friend: "I will not be comforted by one who has not felt the like." We are comforted—that is, made strong —by one who has found the angel of sympathy in the blot of bereavement. Speaking of his mother's sorrow over the death of a son, James Barrie said, "That is how my mother got her soft face, and that is why other mothers ran to her when they lost a child."

III. God's grace gives us deep faith and Christian insight. How many people today resemble Sir Walter Scott who had hoped for an army career until he was left with a slight lameness by illness? Because of his disappointment, he took to reading history, ballads and romances of his native land, and he became the "wizard of romance." He had also hoped to achieve fame as a poet, but he was surpassed by Byron; yet Scott found the angel of compensation after he acknowledged the poetic superiority of his rival. Resentment, rebelliousness and self-pity are demons which destroy what creative capacity we still have after a defeat. But courage, self-understanding and awareness of need may be angels in disguise. Whatever else God's grace may be, it is surely the power given to us to turn blots into angels.

24

Clinic for Broken Hearts

HE HEALETH THE BROKEN IN HEART . . .—PSALM 147:3, KJV.

A Korean woman knocked on the door of a Christian church in her homeland and asked, "Is this where they mend broken hearts?" She had gone to the right place. In a sense every Christian church is a clinic for those suffering from emotional and spiritual heartbreak.

I. In the church, as the fellowship of Christ, we are concerned with what medical men call "preventive treatment."

II. Christianity is a religion of redemption, of recovery of the lost, of renewal for the spiritually exhausted, and of healing for the deeply hurt.

III. How may we be healed by the divine Physician? (A) We must show Him our wound. (B) We must receive His diagnosis and accept His prescription. (C) If our heartbreak is caused by bereavement, we can still live by the power of an endless life, and in the communion of saints we can find our hearts made strong again and our spirits brave. (D) If our heartbreak has almost healed but has left us in chronic anxiety, then we should practice our faith by living a day at a time and by finding God's help at every corner. (E) Favorable prognosis depends on daily visits with our Physician and Lord.

25

Using Those Extra Years

THE RIGHTEOUS. . . . STILL BRING FORTH FRUIT IN OLD
AGE, THEY ARE EVER FULL OF SAP AND GREEN . . .—
PSALM 92:12, 14, RSV.

I. God desires life for us, abundant life and length of days.

II. With the Holy Spirit's aid we shall continue as fighting optimists, for with Christian faith we shall see life and life's problems in true perspective.

III. Don't retire *from* something, but *to* something.

IV. As we grow older we must continue to increase our knowledge of many things in God's world so that we may give ourselves wholeheartedly to God's causes in our generation.

V. Let us remember that the righteous bring forth fruit even in old age—they achieve new victories because they are in a right relationship with reality.

If You'd Only Use Your Imagination!

SON OF MAN, HAVE YOU SEEN WHAT THE ELDERS OF THE
HOUSE OF ISRAEL ARE DOING IN THE DARK, EVERY MAN
IN HIS ROOM OF PICTURES?—EZEKIEL 8:12, RSV.

A lecturer asked members of his class to tell him when they smelled some oil of peppermint he spilled on the floor. Almost instantly half a dozen hands went up. At last the students in the back row smelled the peppermint, too. Then the professor confessed that he had poured water on the floor. How powerful is the imagination! It is so real. Christians should use their imaginations:

I. To visualize what should be done and how it can be accomplished.

II. To put ourselves in the other person's place.

III. To replace pictures of defeat, temptation and evil with those which will be ours when we "Let this mind be in you, which was also in Christ Jesus" (Philippians 2:5, KJV).

II

CHRISTIAN CONVICTIONS

Leave the Ranks of the Uncommitted

... YOU MUST DEDICATE YOURSELVES TO GOD AS MEN
WHO HAVE BEEN BROUGHT FROM DEATH TO LIFE,
DEDICATING YOUR MEMBERS TO GOD FOR THE SERVICE
OF RIGHTEOUSNESS—ROMANS 6:13, MOFFATT.

Commitment one way or the other must be made. We cannot forever drift. If we persist in drifting, we come at last to the point of no return and over the cataract we go. Life gets made up even when our minds do not.

W. Fraser Munro discusses "The Disciple and His Commitment." His emphases provide an illuminating and inspiring outline for a sermon or a series of sermons:[1]

I. *Christian commitment is made to a Person.* It is not made to a program, primarily, nor to an ideology, nor to an abstract way of life, but to a Person. The Person is not a dead hero, but a living Lord. He is history's unique Personality, Jesus Christ. Dr. Munro quotes the answer of St. Irenaeus to Marcion, a second-century heretic. "What new thing did Jesus bring?" asked Marcion. "He brought all that was new in bringing Himself," replied Irenaeus. Full commitment to this new Person makes us new persons.

II. *It is commitment to the will of God.* This commitment is more than submission or pious resignation to the inevitable, as is sometimes stressed in certain hymns. It is an active acceptance of God's daring design. Great Christians have insisted, "Commitment to the will of God means simply the giving of our wills to God."

III. *Commitment to Christ means commitment to the Kingdom of God.* What is this realm? Jesus described it, suggested it and implied it, but He never defined it. It is the Father's kingly rule within us and among us; it is past, present and future. We cannot bring it about, but we can work with God as He brings it to fulfillment.

IV. *Commitment is made to maximum efficiency.* Says Dr. Munro: "The objective of genuine evangelism is not just more

Christians, but more effective Christians." What about our equipment to fight on Christ's side? Are we, as the Army used to say, among the "effectives," or are we part of what the ancient Romans called the "impedimenta"? Not only a football team can be burdened by a man who plays "drawback"!

V. *Commitment is made to spiritual growth.*

VI. *Commitment is made to disciplined living.* Note the link between the words "discipleship" and "discipline." What does discipline involve? When we go all-out for Christ and His cause, we commit ourselves to martyrdom. This is what early leaders meant by "white martyrdom"—"witness," as the original Greek word meant. "Red martyrdom" (death) is rare today in most countries. But "white martyrdom"—witnessing in daily life—is indispensable and imperative. Witnessing may make us unpopular and may create opposition. But the living Lord supplies the armor against all missiles of hostility and He is our Companion on every field of conflict. No martyrdom for Christ is ever wasted.

28

Resources Available

> ... HE IS ABLE TO HELP THOSE WHO ARE TEMPTED—
> HEBREWS 2:18, RSV.

> ... HE IS ABLE FOR ALL TIME TO SAVE THOSE WHO DRAW
> NEAR TO GOD THROUGH HIM ...—HEBREWS 7:25, RSV.

> ... [HE] IS ABLE TO DO FAR MORE ABUNDANTLY THAN
> ALL THAT WE ASK OR THINK ...—EPHESIANS 3:20, RSV.

Help is provided for us and resources are available for meeting the requirements of living here and now.

I. An authentic note of vital Christianity is this: We shall be made adequate to meet life's most difficult demands. We are able? No, but He is able.

II. A marvelous fact about the resources God provides is this: God gives His help before the need is experienced. "Before they call I will answer, while they are yet speaking I will hear" (Isaiah 65:24, RSV).

III. A wonderful truth revealed by Christian experience is this: God makes provision for our growth into spiritual maturity. God came to this planet in the Person of His Son. Knowing our deep need for forgiveness and acceptance, for direction and complete health of body, mind and soul, He gives us Himself—through the Spirit—that we may understand Him better and join Him in serving His grand design.

29

What's the Question? What's the Answer?

IF THE SPIRIT OF HIM WHO RAISED JESUS FROM THE DEAD DWELLS IN YOU, HE . . . WILL GIVE LIFE TO YOUR MORTAL BODIES ALSO THROUGH HIS SPIRIT . . .—ROMANS 8:11, RSV.

When she was dying, Gertrude Stein is said to have roused from a coma to ask anxiously, "What is the *answer?*" Then she lapsed back into unconsciousness. Later still, she roused once more and asked, even more intensely, "What is the *question?*"

On a Sunday in the season hallowed by association with our Lord's pilgrimage to Calvary and beyond, the question may be, "What difference will it make if I become a Christian?" Bishop F. Gerald Ensley has a convincing sermon on the theme, "The Difference Religion Makes."[2]

I. *Religion*—and Bishop Ensley, of course, means the Christian religion—*makes life worth living.* From the perspective of Christian faith, "the universe makes sense." Life is worth living when

it has meaning and when the meaning and purpose furnish moti-
vation. ". . . in thy light shall we see light" (Psalm 36:9, KJV).

II. *Christianity makes men worth loving*. Because God's ap-
praisal of ordinary human beings is so high, we must raise our
estimate. As Bishop Ensley explained:

> Even the lowliest human being has an infinite sacredness as
> God's child. People are not things to be used and, like razor
> blades, thrown away when they lose their sharpness. They are not
> guinea pigs to be made subjects of involuntary experiment. They
> are God's children, to be honored and served for his sake and
> theirs.

Does someone suggest that we can love people for their own sakes,
without a cosmic reference, or that humanism minus theism
prompts high regard, respect and appreciation? What about the
world's "rejects"—the subnormal, the incorrigible and the per-
verted? Can we love our enemies if we do not love God whose
blessed Son said we must love even the worst of our fellow men?
"In the light of God's love for men we find men worth loving."

III. *Christianity renders sacrifice worth making*. Even technological achievement in creating and dispatching successful satellites requires sacrifice. How can we create, with God, a Christian
world order without paying a high price? When I was young,
brash and bold—though quaking in the actual encounter—I de-
bated with Bertrand Russell. A perfect gentleman in all his deal-
ings with me, he displayed impatience only once. I had mentioned
the necessity of sacrifice to make a marriage successful. "I am
tired of hearing Christians talk about sacrifice," he said. "The good
life should not require such self-denial and self-sacrifice."

Tired we may be, but all through life there runs a cross.

> And all through life I see a Cross—
> Where sons of God yield up their breath;
> There is no gain except by loss:
> There is no life except by death;
> There is no vision but by faith.[3]

The cross of Christ is the ground plan of the universe. What it
symbolizes is woven into the texture of existence, even as a red
thread used to be woven into the British Navy rope. Christian
faith assures us that Christ did not die in vain, nor is any sacri-

fice made for Him futilely. After Calvary comes Olivet; following crucifixion is the resurrection. "In the light of God's ultimate triumph, our sacrifices are made worthwhile."

30

The World's Most Powerful Word

SCRIPTURE LESSON—I CORINTHIANS 1:18-25.

What is the most powerful word that can be spoken? Is it the word of a dictator, a judge, a military commander—the word that can mean life or death to a person or an entire community? Is it the word of a medical diagnostician pronouncing a verdict of deliverance from a dreaded disease? Or the opposite verdict? Is it the word of creation? According to a remarkable man who lived centuries ago, a man we know as the Apostle Paul, or Saint Paul, the most powerful word is the word of the cross. To Paul's first readers, the cross was a hideous instrument of tragedy, of punishment, of brutal death. But Paul was not writing about the actual piece of wood, or pieces of wood; nor was he telling the story of Christ's physical sufferings. He wrote about the incredibly Good News that somehow "God was in Christ reconciling the world to himself . . ." (II Corinthians 5:19, RSV). Strangely, this divine-human reconciliation is manifested on the cross of Calvary.

Paul was a realist. He knew there would be two major reactions to this tremendous event which has in it God's own saving action. A wag once observed that mankind is composed of two groups: those who divide mankind into two groups, and those who do not! But Paul's division of human beings is made when they are confronted by the fact of Christ's crucifixion.

I. To one group, in Paul's day and ours, the message or preaching of the cross is foolishness. To use Dr. J. B. Phillips' translation: "The preaching of the Cross is, I know, nonsense to those who are involved in this dying world" (v. 18). Why? To the Jews it was a scandal, a stumbling block, that One who ended life upon a cross could possibly have been God's chosen One, Messiah, Saviour. They could quote their Bible to support their view. Deuteronomy 21:23 declares, ". . . he that is hanged is accursed of God. . ." (kjv). Why did they not ponder Isaiah 53 and realize that God uses the suffering Servant to achieve man's redemption? Moreover death on the cross was not the ceremonial sign the devout Jew believed would follow the arrival of the Messiah. When Paul wrote, there was a crop of alleged messiahs, each claiming to be a wonder worker. But in this Jesus men saw One who was gentle of spirit, who repudiated the spectacular and the sensational, who lived among men as a servant, a slave, and who died the bloody death of a common criminal.

To the Greeks in Paul's day, this message of deliverance from guilt and sin and death and meaninglessness was nonsense, too. Why? They could not believe that God would experience the agony which the Christians knew God felt in the death of his Son Jesus. Greek philosophers were sure that men belittled God by saying that He could be affected by man's actions or pain. God was the Great and Holy. He was detached, disengaged from His creatures' lives. To many persons today it seems incredible and irrelevant to claim that the Power behind and through all things became Man and lived among us. The Christian message was once despised by many Greeks. They desired a wisdom higher than such foolishness. Is it otherwise today with many of us who think we are sophisticated, wise, and intellectually superior to the rank and file?

II. The message of the cross is power unlimited: "Christ nailed to the cross . . . is the power of God and the wisdom of God" (vv. 23-24, neb); "to us who are on the way to salvation it is the power of God" (v. 18, neb). In what sense is it power?

(A) It is God's power to bridge the gulf between Him and us. What made this gulf? Our sin. What bridges it? Reconciliation, at the center of which is forgiveness. (See Ephesians 2:8.) What is power but effectiveness in achieving certain purposes? What is God's purpose? To recover us to full and free and happy membership in His family, to wipe away every trace of our guilt, to achieve a commonwealth in which every nation and every person shall have a significant place and part.

(B) This message of the cross of Christ is the divine wisdom essential to understanding life's meaning and value. Here the preacher would do well to read the exposition by Dr. John Short in *The Interpreter's Bible.*[4]

31

Do We Know Any?

SALUTE THAT TRIED CHRISTIAN, APELLES—ROMANS 16: 10, MOFFATT.

"Mummy," asked a small boy, "what is a Christian?"

"A Christian is a person who loves Christ, believes in Him and follows Him."

The boy blinked, and then asked innocently, "Do we know any?"

A nineteenth-century cynic said that Jesus of Nazareth was the first and last Christian. But each of us knows at least a few people who deserve the name. Here are some identifying marks:

I. A Christian is one who bets his life that Jesus Christ is the chief Clue to basic reality.

II. A Christian is a person who is linked spiritually with other Christians.

III. A Christian is a person who is "under orders."

IV. A Christian cares about others.

32

How Can You Tell a Christian?

I BEAR ON MY BODY THE MARKS OF JESUS—GALATIANS 6:17, RSV.

I. What were these marks or credentials? Paul repeatedly spoke of himself as a bondservant or slave of the Lord Jesus. When others denied that he was, he pointed to his "marks," the scars and wounds he had endured for Jesus' sake and in Christ's service.

II. The true marks of Christ in any followers are inward and spiritual, for the identity of the disciples with the Master must be one of spirit and purpose.

III. The marks of a Christian are an unfaltering and enthusiastic obedience to God's will, an ardent concern to win individuals to the Kingdom, and self-sacrifice. "Christ pleased not himself ..." (Romans 15:3, KJV)—and neither must we.

33

Someone's Watching You

SHOW YOURSELF IN ALL RESPECTS A MODEL OF GOOD
DEEDS, AND IN YOUR TEACHING SHOW INTEGRITY, GRAV-
ITY, AND SOUND SPEECH THAT CANNOT BE CENSURED, SO
THAT AN OPPONENT MAY BE PUT TO SHAME, HAVING
NOTHING EVIL TO SAY OF US—TITUS 2:7-8, RSV.

Too often in church, as in secular circles, we behave as we think we are expected to behave, or we engage in certain activities because others think we should or tell us we should. But the New Testament bids us remember that we must live as Christians. We must be kinder than necessary, heroic in our goodness, honest and deep in our thinking and speaking—because others who are watching us may be influenced by our example.

I. Example is a powerful incentive or deterrent to Christian living. A famous brigade of British Guards, terribly depleted by the retreat from Dunkirk in World War II, came off their battered transports at an English port with unrelaxed discipline:

On the quay they formed up, and marched away as if they had been changing guard. Some of the Frenchmen (lethargic, de-

feated, despairing) looked up listlessly. Slowly in their eyes a
light began to be reborn. Stiffly they arose, squared their shoulders, and marched off after the guards, and before that movement had finished every one of the Frenchmen had fallen in and
was on the march. The power of an example had changed dis-
pirited, defeated men into men who had got back their hope and
their self-respect.[5]

Was it in the story of the Pied Piper of Hamelin that the obser-
vation was made that "everyone pipes for the feet of someone to
follow"? Little boy watches big boy; little girl watches older sister;
child watches adult; pupil observes teacher; teacher scrutinizes
admired leader—thus proceeds the chain reaction of influence-
by-example.

This is why Paul wrote so moralistically about Christian behavior to both Titus (2:7) and Timothy (I, 4:12). Recall the
power of Peter's shadow (Acts 5:15).

II. Jesus is more than a divine Person to be imitated. He is both
food and the hunger for it. He is Saviour as well as Exemplar.
Peter's letter is right: "For to this you have been called, because
Christ also suffered for you, leaving you an example, that you
should follow in his steps" (I Peter 2:21, RSV). Christ expects us to
follow His example. One way is to look to Him for grace and to
remember that others are looking at us. What they see may help
or hinder their own progress toward Christian maturity.

34

Dividends of Discipline

FOR THE MOMENT ALL DISCIPLINE SEEMS PAINFUL
RATHER THAN PLEASANT; LATER IT YIELDS THE PEACE-
FUL FRUIT OF RIGHTEOUSNESS TO THOSE WHO HAVE
BEEN TRAINED BY IT—HEBREWS 12:11, RSV.

TAKE YOUR SHARE OF SUFFERING AS A GOOD SOLDIER OF
CHRIST JESUS—II TIMOTHY 2:3, RSV.

When the word "discipline" is mentioned, not a few respond, "It's for the birds!" It is for the birds! Without the discipline of an instinctive nature, birds could not cope with life. Discipline is also for men and women who would live as mature children of God. According to a dictionary, discipline is "training, especially of the kind which produces self-control, orderliness, obedience and capacity for cooperation." Can we dispense with these qualities in family, state and church?

I. Nothing is learned without struggle and discipline. The first result is pain, but it is not profitless pain. Ask the youngster practicing his piano or violin lesson, while the other neighborhood kids are playing. And ask his family or neighbors if it isn't painful! Paderewski, when told by a queen that he was a genius, had the right explanation: "I may be a genius, but before I became one I was a drudge." You do not ask a chess player to show you how to play the game in a minute. Lifetime study and practice are necessary to mastery. So with proficiency in spiritual engineering—in prayer, in the use of the Bible, in worship and in Christian homemaking.

II. But there are dividends. A pocket diary often contains, under certain dates, two little words: "Dividends Due." On many days dividends are paid to the person who has made discipline a daily practice. What are some of these dividends? Reserve power for a swift demand, and resource for a crisis. What we do at a critical moment is the fruit of long years of discipline. Consider the radio operator on a sinking ship. He continues to the end, sending out signals of the craft's position, not because he is exceptionally brave, but because he is responsible and disciplined. Paul spoke of Christians as soldiers. A soldier is conditioned to obey the commander even if he does not understand the reasons for the command. So must a Christian. And when an emergency breaks, he does not break.

III. Discipline enables us to live daily with what has been called "dust-blown devotion." We ministers often lead undisciplined lives. Our work habits are poor and the organization of our tasks faulty. Too easily our chins go down instead of up. Like the youthful Queen Victoria, we may need a bunch of holly pinned where it will prick us and cause our chins to go up! Better than any such childish spur is the recollection that we are royal kin to the King of all the universe.

IV. A rich dividend of disciplined Christian living is the knowledge that our unwavering fidelity to Christ may rally the ranks of our fellow soldiers. A chaplain in the armed forces lamented to his commander that so many men were casualties in an action which seemed futile. The officer answered, "But chappie, because of what our men did here, the line of the enemy was broken miles away!" Also, being dependable, courageous and loyal brings us into the invigorating comradeship of other gallant servants of God. ". . . be thou faithful unto death . . ." (Revelation 2:10, KJV). Discipline may not "pay off" here, but it will mean that one day you will hear the words, "Well done!"

35

What's in It for Us?

> THEN PETER SPOKE AND SAID TO HIM, "HERE WE HAVE LEFT ALL WE HAD AND FOLLOWED YOU. WHAT ARE WE TO HAVE?"—MATTHEW 19:27, GOODSPEED.

Many persons respond to any appeal with the question, "What's in it for me?" Even the Apostle Peter asked Jesus the question. Were his mixed emotions stirred as he heard the Master make His demand upon the man of property (Matthew 19:16-24)? Certainly Peter and the other disciples had given up everything pagans reckoned to be valuable in order to serve in Christ's task force.

Jesus could have dismissed Peter's question as being irrelevant and selfish. He might have said, "Any person who asks such a question has no idea what following Me means." Instead Jesus, with His unfailing courtesy and understanding, answered Peter. He said, in effect, that the man or woman who sacrifices to share in Christ's campaign will share in Christ's victory. To wear the crown, a man must be willing to bear the cross. Moreover, the Christian soldier will receive far more than he gives up, although the rewards for valor in Christ's service will be spiritual and, therefore, more enduring than material prizes. The Christian will have eternal life with all its marvelous surprises.

"What are we to have?"

I. *Comfort.* This is not precisely the same as comfortableness. Divine disturbance accompanies commitment to God's Kingdom, but there will be the deep comfort of knowing that our sin is forgiven, and that in spite of our failings we are accepted by God whose love is pure, holy and transforming. "Come to me, all who labor and are heavy laden, and I will give you rest" (Matthew 11:28, RSV). Jesus speaks comfortable words to our condition. He shares the yoke with us, and we find the load lighter. Our shoulders and hearts are no longer sore. He gives us the assurance that all is well for those who put their trust in Him, who follow and obey Him.

II. *A cross.* Samuel Rutherford, eighteenth-century Scottish minister and saint, said, "If you have not got a cross, you have not got Christ, for it is one of the first of His gifts." A cross is a voluntarily accepted burden. A cross is a load you may evade, an obligation you may escape, a cause you are not compelled to support except by your enlightened and sensitized conscience. Everyone knows what his cross may be; every Christian knows that shouldering his cross, for Christ's sake and the gospel's, brings Christ near. Interracial understanding, world peace, adequate housing for low-income families, Christian unity and advance on every frontier, Christian education and evangelism everywhere in the inhabited world, and reclamation of juvenile delinquents—how many causes wait for Christians to get under them and behind them!

III. *Companionship.* A Christian is a person who has been admitted to a new, divine fellowship. Eternal life is life in God. Commit yourself to God in Christ and you will be united to the love of God in Christ. Nothing can separate you from this love. But the Christian also knows the fellowship of other good companions of Christ. Is there a city or a village in which the Christian cannot find a company of friends?

IV. *Certainty.* Much will remain tentative to the end of the road here, but of some facts we can be sure: ". . . I know whom I have believed . . ." (II Timothy 1:12, RSV); ". . . I know that my redeemer liveth . . ." (Job 19:25, KJV); ". . . we know that all things work together for good to them that love God . . ." (Romans 8:28, KJV); "I know that in our Father's house are many abiding places, that because he lives we too shall live, that there will be reunion with all in Christ beyond earth's separations" (John 14:2, AUTHOR'S PARAPHRASE); "The kingdom of the world has become the kingdom of our Lord and of his Christ, and he shall reign for ever and ever" (Revelation 11:15, RSV).

Do We Need Forgiveness?

SCRIPTURE LESSON—II KINGS 5:1-14; EPHESIANS 2:4-10;
MARK 2:1-12.

Do we need forgiveness? Some of our contemporaries think we
need only to adjust to our failures, whatever they may be. Others
say that if we need forgiveness, and if God exists, then we shall
have it, or we do have it. Still others say that while we may need
pardon, we shall only experience the pardon granted us by the
person or persons we have hurt, and the pardon we give ourselves. In the gospel story of the paralyzed man brought to Jesus
by loyal friends, certain truths are underscored.

I. Much of our trouble comes from a sense of guilt. The patient
and friends and spectators at the Master's "clinic" expected that
Jesus would deal with the paralysis, but not by treating the man's
spiritual condition. "My son, your sins are forgiven" (Mark 2:5,
RSV), said Jesus, with the insight which uncovered the relation of
the physical distress to the spiritual disease. No one would claim
that moral factors contribute to all sickness, but few would deny
that emotional and spiritual distress can affect bodily functions
and general health. Who does not know what it is to have a sense
of guilt? Not necessarily morbid or neurotic guilt, but what some
would call "existential" guilt feelings from being involved in the
misery, the war climate, the injustice of our human situation.
Scan the newspaper headlines; watch the telecast news; look into
your own heart. Is there nothing for which we need to be forgiven?

II. Deep forgiveness must come from God. Human beings must
grant forgiveness to each other, but the ultimate source of pardon
is beyond them. Some of the lawyers who were shocked at Jesus'
assurance of forgiveness were at least right in saying, "Who can
forgive sins but God alone?" (Mark 2:7, RSV). Their blindness and
mistake consisted in failing to realize that in Jesus Christ, God
was actively present, forgiving the patient's sins. ". . . there is
forgiveness with thee, that thou mayest be feared," says the Bible
(Psalm 130:4, KJV). And we would add, "and that thou mayest
be loved."

III. God's forgiveness is His gift. We do not deserve it and we cannot earn it. But we can receive it as our lives are opened, and our minds and wills changed from love of the evil way to desire for the more excellent way. "For it is by His grace you are saved, through trusting Him; it is not your own doing. It is God's gift, not a reward for work done. There is nothing for anyone to boast of. For we are God's handiwork, created in Christ Jesus to devote ourselves to the good deeds for which God has designed us" (Ephesians 2:8-10, NEB).

IV. God's forgiveness becomes real and accessible as we keep Jesus Christ and His cross steadily in sight. Like the pilgrim in Bunyan's *Pilgrim's Progress,* in imaginative faith we take our place on Calvary, and the burden of our sins rolls away and we see it no more. We ourselves, with so much forgiven, become forgiving, loving; and we engage in Christ's work. No sermon on this central truth can fail to be enriched by the simple gospel hymn "There Is a Green Hill Far Away."[6]

37

You Belong!

... ALL BELONGS TO YOU; ... LIFE, DEATH, THE PRESENT AND THE FUTURE—ALL BELONGS TO YOU; AND YOU BELONG TO CHRIST, AND CHRIST TO GOD—1 CORINTHIANS 3:21-23, MOFFATT.

I. To be a Christian is to belong, and to know that you belong to God.

II. To be a Christian is to belong to the one society which transcends time—and all racial, temperamental, social and political differences. This society is the church of the living God.

III. To be a Christian is to belong to Christ, and to all everywhere in every era who have put their trust in Him. World communion means little if it does not enable us to realize, at ever deeper levels, that all belongs to us and we belong to all that in Christ is eternal, human and divine, enriching and liberating.

Faith With a Built-in Doubt

"I DO BELIEVE," THE BOY'S FATHER BURST OUT. "HELP
ME TO BELIEVE MORE!"—MARK 9:24, PHILLIPS.

Louis Binstock tells of a man, financially secure, with position
and prestige, who confessed to his rabbi that he had nothing for
which to live. He would not take "the same, old-time bunk—
'Have faith in the Lord'—and presto! all your troubles are over,
and life is beautiful forever afterward." The rabbi insisted that
the man help himself by using the great storehouse of spiritual
power God has placed within every soul. He told the old Chinese
story of the little fish who had heard that without water no living
creature could survive. The little fish swam frantically from pond
to river to ocean in search of water, until a wise old fish convinced
him he had been in water since the day he was born. The little
fish began the long swim home and said, "I had water all the time,
and I didn't know it." So with faith, the gift of God. If people
question this "built-in" faith, let them ask themselves how many
times they have actually used faith.

I. We use faith automatically. It is only when we confront
strange, more demanding and critical situations in which we must
consciously employ this force that we shrink back. Faith as a
principle is one thing; a faith, or set of beliefs, is another. Beliefs
do matter, but mere intellectual assent to these beliefs may not
affect our living. The experience of the epileptic boy's father, first
with the disciples, who let him down, and subsequently with
Jesus, is pertinent. The key word is "trust." Trust means to lean
upon, with our whole weight.

II. Faith, as distinguished from belief, requires us to lean our
whole weight, our whole concern and personality, upon the one
trusted. Paul Tillich has described faith as "an ultimate concern
that demands a total surrender of the personality." Our ultimate
concern must not be any thing or any one less than the Highest—
God. We must not give to any means-to-the-end the loyalty and
veneration that belong solely to God.

Going to church helps to remove roadblocks to dynamic use of the faith God gives us. The church is composed of seekers and finders of the divine Ultimate; in their company we are invited and helped to plunge in over our heads and hearts.

III. Dynamic faith in God through Christ permits an element of uncertainty. Only those with secure basic faith can doubt many secondary or peripheral matters. Faith is not to be confused with credulity. We do not know all the answers, but we know Christ; or rather, He knows us and we believe in Him. One observer says that most of us have so little faith that we have refused to doubt; or if we do doubt, we have guilty feelings. In the Bible and in contemporary life, God never frowns upon honest doubt. He proves Himself to us as we bet our lives on Him. Verification comes through commitment, and our experience of His reality. If we do His will, we shall know; but always with the certainty will be the uncertainty, the risk, and the "built-in" doubt.

39

Too Good Not to Be True

GOD IS LOVE, AND HE WHO ABIDES IN LOVE ABIDES IN GOD, AND GOD ABIDES IN HIM—I JOHN 4:16, RSV.

GOD SENT HIS ONLY SON INTO THE WORLD, SO THAT WE MIGHT LIVE THROUGH HIM—I JOHN 4:9, RSV.

WE KNOW THAT WE HAVE PASSED OUT OF DEATH INTO LIFE, BECAUSE WE LOVE THE BRETHREN—I JOHN 3:14, RSV.

We speak of things that seem too good to be true, but what about the things in life which are too good not to be true?

I. Too good not to be true is faith's central affirmation that God is love.

II. Too good not to be true is God's self-disclosure and self-giving in Christ.

III. Too good not to be true is Christ's love operating through us, bringing life in place of death, here and now as well as hereafter.

40

Prayer in Three Dimensions

OPEN THOU MINE EYES, THAT I MAY BEHOLD WONDROUS THINGS OUT OF THY LAW. . . . INCLINE MY HEART UNTO THY TESTIMONIES. . . . ORDER MY STEPS IN THY WORD . . .—PSALM 119:18, 36, 133, KJV.

These petitions express deep needs of the Christian traveler.

I. "Open thou mine eyes. . . ." Help me to see the beauty and order of the world that God has made, and continues to make. Open mine eyes to see the unlimited possibilities for growth of character in human beings. Open mine eyes to see that God guides and guards His children, and that He has come in Christ to save us.

> O may no earthborn cloud arise
> To hide Thee from Thy servant's eyes.[7]

II. "Incline my heart. . . ." Create in me the desire for the highest that the opened eyes of faith are enabled to see. Who, after examining his own desires, can deny that within us is resistance to the highest? Otherwise, why the good that we would do we do not, and the evil we would not do we do? But if God can open the eyes of the blind, He can transform my desire.

> Bend the stubborn will to Thine,
> Melt the cold with fire divine,
> Erring hearts to right incline.[8]

III. "Order my steps . . . ." The Revised Standard Version translates the words: "Keep steady my steps according to thy promise, and let no iniquity get dominion over me."

(A) Is it not true that even when we see the way we should take, and have the desire and will to take it, we waver and wobble, stagger and stumble? A nineteenth-century Scottish preacher prayed, "Lord, hold me on a steady pace." Christ steadies the shaky soul. He guides and supports us, as we support the little ones entrusted to our care.

(B) Order my steps so that I go into the areas of human need. Let me not hesitate when Christian discipleship leads me into a battle for justice, brotherhood and peace. And when I walk in slippery places, hold me fast. A Latin motto reads, "I hold, and I am held." Said a noble pastor to an old friend and parishioner, "Well, Donald, how are you keeping?" "I'm not keeping," said the other with a gentle smile, "I am kept." Christ is able "to keep you from falling and to present you without blemish before the presence of his glory with rejoicing . . ." (Jude 24, RSV).

41

Three Ways You Can Pray

> WHAT AM I TO DO? I WILL PRAY WITH THE SPIRIT AND
> I WILL PRAY WITH THE MIND ALSO . . .—I CORINTHIANS
> 14:15, RSV.

Without attempting to answer the intellectual questions concerning prayer in a world of law, intelligent persons can tell you that prayer changes things. Difficulties remain, but those who pray seem to tap sources of power; and non-praying persons do not. Men "ought always to pray," said Jesus, "and not lose heart" (Luke 18:1, RSV). Nevertheless, we ask with the Apostle Paul: "What am I to do? I will pray with the spirit and I will pray with the mind also." But how? Are there some ways we modern men and women can pray that will introduce to us the divine Lord we seek to know better? How can prayer enable us to release power for good in the lives of others?

I. Pray affirmatively. This does not mean autosuggestion, but prayer from men and women who believe that God lives and that He is absolute goodness, love, wisdom and power. To pray affirmatively is not to assert piously that anything we desire will be, or is being, granted. Who can say that to one incurably afflicted? To pray affirmatively is to come with boldness, not timidity, to God. He waits for us to clear the channel. We can, as the ancient hymn "Te Deum" declares, acknowledge God to be the Lord, the Ruler of men, and the Governor of the universe. When we pray with such faith, we open our lives to the Spirit and help Him open other lives to His cleansing and strengthening influence.

II. We can pray for direction. Most of the time we know what road to take or what course to choose. Inevitably, however, times come when the choice between two "goods" is difficult. God does not send celestial telegrams to point the way, but God does give guidance when we bring our minds and souls to Him. To pray with the mind and understanding is to help God help us to find the beam we must travel. William E. Sangster reminds us that God guides us through the Bible, through our reason, through the church, through circumstances; He guides us by our conscience and also by the inner light. Appeal to the inner light is made through prayer.

III. We can pray with the spirit and the understanding, which means that we pray unselfishly. The most unselfish prayer is "intercessory," which comes from two Latin words meaning "to go between." We go between the vast power of God and the need of a fellow human being, and link them. No human glory attaches to this kind of prayer, for the intercessor works in secret and his enormous service to the community is known only to God. Muriel Lester says she was greatly fortified during difficult days in World War II when she read a postscript in a letter from a loyal friend: "I am holding you up to the light." "When I think of you, I think of you and God," read another letter. We do not tell God what to do for another, but we do ask God to use us and our prayers as instruments of His loving purpose. Every day we can think of God and others together.

Private Business

> ... WHEN YOU PRAY, GO INTO YOUR OWN ROOM, SHUT
> YOUR DOOR AND PRAY TO YOUR FATHER PRIVATELY.
> YOUR FATHER WHO SEES ALL PRIVATE THINGS WILL
> REWARD YOU—MATTHEW 6:6, PHILLIPS.

I. Thinking of this essential "private business," we note that each person must live a secret inner life.

II. Only One knows the whole secret of our selves.

III. Christ admits us to the divine secret—knowledge of the Father.

Making a New Beginning Through Prayer

> SURELY YOU CAN'T BE SO IDIOTIC AS TO THINK THAT A
> MAN BEGINS HIS SPIRITUAL LIFE IN THE SPIRIT AND
> THEN COMPLETES IT BY REVERTING TO OUTWARD OB-
> SERVANCES?—GALATIANS 3:4, PHILLIPS.

Every normal person has to make a fresh start in life from time to time. Satisfaction with present achievement spells stagnation, and stagnation signifies slipping backward. This is particularly true in the development for Christian witness and other forms of Christian service.

I. To make a new beginning, we must pray by following the example of Christ who focused His prayers on God.

II. In prayer, we must not only thank God for His mercy and pardon, but also proceed to find through prayer and worshipful meditation what God would have us be and do.

III. ". . . life in the Spirit . . ."—life continually nourished and clarified by prayer—will help us to plan our lives.

IV. A new beginning in God through prayer, which is faith becoming articulate and dynamic, will be followed by the grace of continuance.

44

Make These Adjustments

PRAY THEN LIKE THIS: OUR FATHER WHO ART IN HEAVEN—MATTHEW 6:9, RSV.

Contained within the disciples' prayer are revelations, insights and principles by which we can live at maximum effectiveness. To live greatly, we must make essential adjustments—not once, but continuously. What are some of these adjustments?

I. Adjustment to reality. The first three petitions in this prayer relate to God and His glory, and the following three concern human needs and relationships. God is given priority and supremacy; thereafter, and only then, do we turn to our needs. To pray and live by "Our Father who art in heaven" is to establish our relationship to basic reality.

II. Adjustment to the world of nature and of persons follows from the adjustment to reality. How easily we think of the world as hostile, and of people as predatory and unfriendly. But if this world is organized by righteous, Fatherly love—not for our comfort, but for our training and growth toward maturity—others are our fellow students, good, bad and indifferent, for all are members of one Father's household.

III. Adjustment to self follows from true use of the prayer. Who doesn't on occasion hate himself, and disparage his God-given personality, and long for another? Wrote Mark Rutherford: "Blessed are those who give us back our self-respect." God does that for His children when they realize that they are of royal blood.

45

Engage in This Enterprise

THY KINGDOM COME, THY WILL BE DONE, ON EARTH AS IT IS IN HEAVEN—MATTHEW 6:10, RSV.

The Kingdom of God is God's Fatherly rule over all of life. It is the realm of right relationships. Jesus spoke of it in three ways: the Kingdom has come, the Kingdom is coming and the Kingdom will come. In the Person of the King of love, the Lord Jesus, the realm has arrived. With His advent, the powers of the commonwealth have come and are now available to every person of faith. It is therefore within us, among us, and in our midst. It is here, but not in its fullness. The Kingdom is God's; therefore it is not "up to us." Yet our co-operation is required for its realization.

I. Engage in this Kingdom-building enterprise with God's Spirit because the Kingdom's fullness has not yet come.

II. Engage in this tremendous and continuing task, with and within Christ's church.

III. Pray these petitions in the confidence of ultimate victory, for He must reign; and although we must not minimize the power of evil in our world, divine defeat is unthinkable.

Travel This Two-Way Street

AND FORGIVE US OUR DEBTS, AS WE ALSO HAVE FOR-
GIVEN OUR DEBTORS—MATTHEW 6:12, RSV.

I. Pray this prayer only when you realize that you need to ask for forgiveness, and need to be forgiving.

II. Pray this prayer only if you meet the condition attached, for, as a New Testament expositor says, we are praying, "Forgive us our sins in proportion as we forgive those who have sinned against us."

III. Only Christ can make us fit to pray this prayer. Only His love within us, beamed from us, can make us forgiving and thereby prepare us for God's forgiveness.

Join This Resistance Movement

AND LEAD US NOT INTO TEMPTATION, BUT DELIVER US
FROM EVIL—MATTHEW 6:13, RSV.

World War II, and subsequent international crises, disclosed the necessity as well as the hazards of resistance movements. Virtue should be positive, but being against something does not necessarily mean that we are aggressively for its opposite. Nevertheless, great living does not develop from taking the well-known line of least resistance. Amiable acquiescence may be moral cowardice. Compliance often denotes spiritual weakness.

Thus, in the prayer, which not only teaches us to pray but contains a design for great living, Christ asks us to join a resistance movement. We are to enlist through asking God for power to move away from evil, however alluring. We are to fight an enemy, the enemy designated by the Bible as "the evil one" (I John 2:13, RSV). However uncomfortable it is for most of us to think of evil personified, Scripture describes evil not as an abstract force or principle but as an active, personal power opposed to God. (Exegesis supports the translation, "deliver us from the evil one.") Whatever frustrates God's purpose, and whatever is anti-man and anti-God, we are to resist. We may profitably forget about academic discussions relating to the origin of evil. When the house is on fire, a monograph on the origin of house fires is no help. Firefighting is!

I. God does not tempt us, but He allows us to be tested. (See James 1:12-17.) It is unthinkable that the God we know in Christ, and through Christ, would try to make His human children do anything wrong. But to face trial is, or may be, good for us. Planes must have test pilots. Souls too must be examined and subjected to strain. So a paraphrase by Dr. Hugh Martin gives meaning and force to what our Lord said: "Do not allow us to be subjected to the ordeal of trial and suffering, but if we must face it, give us strength to endure and remain faithful."

Temptation is part of living, and there is no sin in temptation itself. Was not Jesus tempted? "My son, if thou come to serve the Lord, prepare thy soul for temptation. Set thy heart aright, and constantly endure" (Ecclesiasticus 2:1-2, KJV). Whether we think of temptation as testing or as evil's enticement, it need not cause disaster. Tribulation means threshing. Threshing separates wheat from chaff. A nation's fiercest testing or threshing may be its glory. Winston Churchill said of his own nation in its darkest days, "This was their finest hour." Is it otherwise in spiritual warfare?

II. God wants us to see temptation for what it is, but not to be foolhardy in dealing with it. Therefore we need divine help. With such help our resistance movement is bound to win. Escape from the enemy and victory over him will be costly. Lent reminds us, as does every replica of Christ's cross, that the struggle cost Christ His life. But Christ became the victor. "And lead us not into temptation, but deliver us from evil." To commit ourselves to our heavenly Father and to His cause in the world—to make His will ours—is to be given positive power and effective weapons for the battle against evil.

III. What are the weapons in the armory of Christ? (A) Self-respect. For Biblical illustration, consider Nehemiah 6:11: "Should such a man as I flee?" (rsv). Some things a man will not do, particularly if he is "a man in Christ" (II Corinthians 12:2, rsv). (B) Tradition is a defensive weapon. Pericles appealed to his fellow citizens to remember that they were Athenians, and rallied his own courage by the reminder that he too belonged to a great company. (C) Others—their confidence and love—keep a man strong in resistance to the worst. What if someone's heart is broken by my defection? What if my easy tolerance of racial hatred, of corporate dishonesty, or of some social injustice, depresses and otherwise hurts others? (D) Most powerful of all weapons is Christ's presence. He is the invisible Commander of all the forces of goodness and truth. ". . . lo, I am with you always . . ." (Matthew 28:20, rsv). Never underrate the forces of Christ, nor His own power through the Holy Spirit. Childlike they may seem, but mature men and women know the wisdom of the old gospel hymn:

> Ask the Saviour to help you,
> Comfort, strengthen, and keep you;
> He is willing to aid you;
> He will carry you through.[9]

48

The Power and the Glory

FOR THINE IS THE KINGDOM, AND THE POWER, AND THE
GLORY, FOREVER. AMEN—MATTHEW 6:13, KJV.

Not all of the oldest manuscripts of the gospel contain these words, although the footnote in the Revised Standard Version states that some do. Whether it is original or not, long association, at least in Protestant churches, makes this doxology seem an integral part of the prayer. In the early Christian centuries it came into liturgical use, and it may have been a response sung by the worshipers to their leader.

I. This ascription proclaims that victory belongs to God and not to evil. On Palm Sunday, in Holy Week, and in every dark hour, this truth needs to be broadcast: The Lord God omnipotent reigneth. A victory has been won in advance. Death and evil do not have the final word. "Art thou a king then?" asked the Roman governor, Pilate (John 18:37, KJV). One crowned with thorns, scourged, spat upon, rejected and crucified between two common criminals, did not look regal. But of His Kingdom there shall be no end, for God was in Christ and God is in Christ. And of this strange King of love we may say, with David: "Thine, O Lord, is the greatness, and the power, and the glory, and the victory, and the majesty: . . . thine is the kingdom, O Lord, and thou art exalted as head above all" (I Chronicles 29:11, KJV). Like a seal to the prayer is the word "forever," literally "for all ages." In this word we may have a protest against the heresy that there is no future world. As Ernest F. Scott wrote, "The God whom we worship now will be sovereign in all ages and in all worlds." Could you not find in the Palm Sunday story the insights to support this faith? Certainly the eyes of Christian faith look through and beyond the last week before Christ's death to Easter morning and the community of the resurrection, which is the church.

II. This must be the church's response to God's action and design for his children. When this ascription was added to the prayer, perhaps as early as the second century, the time was one of darkness for the young church. But this grand affirmation reflected their undaunted faith, even when it was hard to pray with assurance, "Thy kingdom come, thy will be done on earth as it is in heaven."

Such faith demands our response. Will the future be God's or the devil's? The devil had a plausible claim that the kingdom, power and glory belong to him (Luke 4:5-6), but the Lord is King for ever and ever (Psalm 10:16). We have seen the Kingdom come, and we see it coming in Christ.

Share the Wealth

FOR IF THE GENTILES HAVE HAD A SHARE IN THE JEWS'
SPIRITUAL "GOOD THINGS" IT IS ONLY FAIR THAT THEY
SHOULD LOOK AFTER THE JEWS AS FAR AS THE GOOD
THINGS OF THIS WORLD ARE CONCERNED—ROMANS 15:
27, PHILLIPS.

I. Share your wealth of ability and talent with others.

II. Share your profits with God, and so win other members of
His human family.

III. Share your wealth in Christ with your brothers and sisters
in this community and throughout the earth.

More Blessed to Receive—Sometimes

I ALWAYS THANK MY GOD FOR THE GRACE OF GOD THAT
HAS BEEN BESTOWED ON YOU IN JESUS CHRIST; IN HIM
YOU HAVE RECEIVED A WEALTH OF ALL BLESSING, FULL
POWER TO SPEAK OF YOUR FAITH AND FULL INSIGHT
INTO ITS MEANING, ALL OF WHICH VERIFIES THE TESTI-
MONY WE BORE TO CHRIST WHEN WE WERE WITH YOU.
THUS YOU LACK NO SPIRITUAL ENDOWMENT DURING
THESE DAYS OF WAITING TILL OUR LORD JESUS CHRIST IS
REVEALED . . .—I CORINTHIANS 1:4-7, MOFFATT.

Giving is essential to Christian living. Christian stewardship is
not an elective in Christ's school, but a required lifetime course.

Paul laid down a principle of life to the elders of the church: "It is more blessed to give than to receive" (Acts 20:35, RSV). But the Apostle also said, in substance, that it is blessed to receive. In his letter to the Corinthians he speaks of "spiritual endowment," a bestowal, and "a wealth of all blessing."

The text suggests three ideas. In receiving Christ, you receive: (A) a wealth of blessing; (B) full power to speak your faith by witnessing in words, and in the quality of life you manifest in your home, your job and your citizenship; and (C) "full insight into its meaning"; for when your mind has been set afire by the Spirit of Christ, who is the Spirit of Truth, you think beyond your normal capacity, and both insight and understanding increase.

51

Say the Secret Word—and Live By It

> FOR BY GRACE YOU HAVE BEEN SAVED THROUGH FAITH; AND THIS IS NOT YOUR OWN DOING, IT IS THE GIFT OF GOD . . .—EPHESIANS 2:8, RSV.
>
> BY THE GRACE OF GOD I AM WHAT I AM, AND HIS GRACE TOWARD ME WAS NOT IN VAIN—I CORINTHIANS 15:10, RSV.

"Say the secret word and win—." Christians, too, have a secret word or a secret energy by which they can conquer what seems to be unconquerable, and can be sustained under what appear to be intolerably heavy loads. The word, a key word in the New Testament, is *grace*.

I. What does grace mean? Grace characterizes a poised person. Grace is part of an ecclesiastical title: "Your Grace." Grace is a blessing before or after a meal. Grace is extra time given for the payment of an obligation. Derived from a Greek word meaning "a lovely thing," grace refers to physical beauty, winsomeness and charm. In the Bible, grace means both a gift that is undeserved and unpurchasable, and an energy. Said an old preacher, "Divine affection rolling toward the shores of human need—this is grace."

II. Three expressions of grace will help us to live more meaningfully: (A) the grace of God's creativity, or what Paul calls "this grace wherein we stand . . ." (Romans 5:2, KJV); (B) the redemptive grace of God, focused in Jesus Christ, wherein forgiveness is realized at the center of one's personality; and (C) conquering grace, wherein we are made more than conquerors over every sin and failure.

52

You Can't Live Without Him

SCRIPTURE LESSON—ACTS 19:1-6, RSV.

Twelve men interviewed by Paul shocked him when they admitted that they had never heard about the Holy Spirit. They were religious men. Early Christians found it almost inconceivable that anyone claiming to be one of them had not experienced and recognized the Spirit's activity. Why? Because Christians cannot live the Christian way without the Holy Spirit. He is indeed the presence, pervasive and powerful, of God Himself.

The Spirit is manifest in usual, normal, everyday occurrences even more than in unusual phenomena. True, we have records of unusual phenomena, ranging from strange linguistic ability to flights into the ecstatic. But our gospel assures us that "we must see the gift of the Spirit not as mysterious, limited, sporadic and spectacular, but as a constant and natural activity working through the whole church."[10]

W. Gordon Robinson has translated I Corinthians 12:4-6 in these suggestive words:

> There are varieties of gifts, but the same Spirit. And there are varieties of service, but the same Lord. And there are varieties

of dynamic activities, but the same God who activates everything in everyone.[11]

Here are Dr. Robinson's main points in his discussion of the Holy Spirit's pervasive activity:

I. The Holy Spirit gives gifts to all His people, and differing gifts to different recipients. (See I Corinthians 12:7-11, 28-30, RSV.)

II. The Holy Spirit is the "inspiration of all service in the church and to the community." (See I Corinthians 12:5, 27; Ephesians 4:3, RSV.)

III. The Holy Spirit is the promoter of all our activities, "the varieties of service." Some are extraordinary; others are normal. We see His work in worship (I Corinthians 12:3; 14:1-8, RSV); in prayer (Romans 8:26-27; I Corinthians 14:15, RSV); in missionary service (Acts 11:28-29, RSV). We see the Spirit's operations in producing Christian personalities, as the harvest of the Spirit attests in Galatians 5:22 (RSV). What is the Christian way of living? It is what Galatians 5:25 (RSV) calls "walking by the Spirit."

53

The Spirit Writes in Shorthand

I HAVE SAID THIS TO YOU IN FIGURES; THE HOUR IS COMING WHEN I SHALL NO LONGER SPEAK TO YOU IN FIGURES BUT TELL YOU PLAINLY OF THE FATHER. . . . WHEN THE SPIRIT OF TRUTH COMES, HE WILL GUIDE YOU INTO ALL THE TRUTH. . . . HE WILL TAKE WHAT IS MINE AND DECLARE IT TO YOU—JOHN 16:25, 13-14, RSV.

A camel has been described as a horse put together by a committee. Our concept of God frequently resembles a committee's work. Over the Taj Mahal in India are inscribed the seventy-seven Arabic names for God. We are not Arabs, but we have nearly as many names for Him, ranging from "Principles of Concretion" to "the Man Upstairs." *Time* reported Robert Frost as saying:

> God seems to me to be something which wants us to win. In tennis. Or poetry. Or marriage. I'm like a modern car in religious matters. I may look convertible, but I'm a hardtop.[12]

God—Something, Some One—wants us to win. God is Spirit and the Highest Authority. God is like Christ, said the men who knew Him best. "God was in Christ . . ." (II Corinthians 5:19, RSV), declared the Apostle Paul. If our concept of God seems inconsistent, intricate and unsatisfying, it may be as it should be. God defined would be God confined; God confined would be God finished. Thus in His self-disclosure God must use shorthand.

I. Much of life has to be written in a kind of shorthand. "In divinity as in love, what's best worth saying cannot be said"[13] in words alone. Words themselves are symbols, shorthand for meaning and for truth. Science uses shorthand constantly, from water as H_2O to Einstein's formula. Margaret Applegarth reminds us that in His superb teaching Jesus used names for Himself that hold "physical mysteries in shorthand and similar patterns of spiritual meanings to be painted on the world of the eyeball." Consider "bread," "water of life," and "door." Why should it repel fastidious folks today to be told at the communion service to "feed on Him in thy heart by faith"? Do we not find spiritual sustenance in "feeding" upon a great book, or drinking in liberating music, or in art and friendship?

II. The Bible is a kind of shorthand. The Holy Spirit helps our minds to transcribe it into messages from God to ourselves and our world.

III. The so-called natural world is supernatural because through it God speaks to us of His greatness in creative power, of His wisdom and dependability, and of His orderliness and beauty. Much in nature dismays and appalls: tornadoes, earthquakes, cobras and cancer. But can we not discern in the beauty of the universe around us something of God's marvelous artistry, and even through the myriad sounds of today's world hear something of God's voice?

IV. Christ—His life, His teaching, and above all His cross and resurrection—is God's shorthand for His love unfailing, unconditional, and unfathomable.

God: Idea or Experience?

THIS IS THE TRUE GOD AND ETERNAL LIFE—I JOHN 5:20, RSV.

I KNOW WHOM I HAVE BELIEVED . . .—II TIMOTHY 1:12, RSV.

WE KNOW THAT IN EVERYTHING GOD WORKS FOR GOOD WITH THOSE WHO LOVE HIM, WHO ARE CALLED ACCORD-ING TO HIS PURPOSE—ROMANS 8:28, RSV.

Is God an idea, a notion, an intellectual concept, or is He a reality experienced in your life? Ideas are important. The idea of God is one of the most sublime, yet sometimes one of the most degrading, entertained by the mind of man. How we think about reality is relevant to how we behave. Even more relevant is our experience of God. Consider three New Testament certainties derived from a rich experience of God.

I. God has come in Jesus Christ and we have been given sufficient knowledge of the divine character and design to go on our way with God, confident that the end is sure and must be right.

II. God will support and sustain us in every situation.

III. We can know "that all things work together for good to them that love God . . ." (Romans 8:28, KJV). Not everything works together for the best, or for our happiness, but the person who loves God has His aid and interest in whatever he does.

IV. How can we experience God and know with deep conviction that He has visited this world in the Person of His Son? (A) Follow the light provided by Christian counselors, the church, God's Word, prayer, and Bible reading. (B) Keep Jesus Christ constantly in sight.

Is God Your Private Secretary?

MY FATHER, IF IT BE POSSIBLE, LET THIS CUP PASS
FROM ME; NEVERTHELESS, NOT AS I WILL, BUT AS THOU
WILT—MATTHEW 26:39, RSV.

Florence Nightingale, a colorful and exceedingly competent person, is described by one of her biographers, Lytton Strachey, in these words:

> Her conception of God was certainly not orthodox. She felt towards Him as she might have felt towards a glorified sanitary engineer; and in some of her speculations she seems hardly to distinguish between the Deity and the drains. As one turns over these singular pages [of her diary], one has the impression that Miss Nightingale has got the Almighty into her clutches, and that, if He is not careful, she will kill Him with overwork.[14]

Miss Nightingale seems to have been aware of this tendency in her thinking, for she made this note in her diary: "I *must* [and she underlined *must*] remember that God is not my private secretary." Nor is God our private secretary.

I. We cannot dictate to Him.

II. We cannot expect God to agree with our views of people, issues, and right and wrong.

Refer to God

... THEY ... LIMITED THE HOLY ONE OF ISRAEL—
PSALM 78:41, KJV.

When Stanley Baldwin was Prime Minister of the United Kingdom, he made an important speech in the House of Commons. Afterwards, his secretary picked up his notes and found one that read: "Refer again to A.G." He was puzzled. What did it mean? Next day, the secretary discovered that the Prime Minister meant, "Refer again to Almighty God." We need to ask what or who is the God to whom we refer.

I. We limit God by unworthy thoughts about His character and activity. Consider the person who insists the minister baptize a critically ill infant because he believes that if the child should die he would miss salvation. We believe in the importance of baptism, but we do not believe God would condemn an innocent child because certain ritualistic or ceremonial requirements had not been fulfilled. Consider also the person who thinks God always sends suffering to punish wrongdoing. Job's problem recurs today.

II. We limit God by our reference to Him as the God of our nation or race. We may disavow any such concept of a tribal deity, but consider our behavior. The God in whom we really believe is the God we disclose by our attitudes and actions. If God is our Father, He is the Father of all men everywhere. If He loves white Protestant Americans, he loves Negroes, Germans, Russians, Japanese, and every nation or racial group. "It is," as Benjamin Mays wrote, "all or nothing." God is our Father, and we are all brethren.

III. We limit God by referring to Him as if He made Himself known and changed lives only according to a particular pattern. After hearing an evangelist speak, a man's deep peace was disturbed by anxieties about his wife, whom he deeply loved and who had recently died. He talked to Townley Lord about it. "She never had such an experience as I have had, although she was truly good and Christian in spirit." Dr. Lord told him that God can be trusted, and he quoted the wonderful verse in Hebrews 6:10-12, as translated by James Moffatt: "God is not unfair; he will not forget what you have done, nor the love you have shown for his sake in ministering. . . ." The author of Hebrews was affirming that God notes the difference between good and evil actions and attitudes. His ways are not as our ways. A valid spiritual experience does not imply that another type of experience is not also God's device and instrument.

Contact!

SHE HAD HEARD THE REPORTS ABOUT JESUS, AND CAME
UP BEHIND HIM IN THE CROWD AND TOUCHED HIS GAR-
MENT—MARK 5:27, RSV.

I. We make contact with God through the living, visible
garment of our Creator—the beauty of the natural world.

II. We make contact with God through the Son of His love,
Jesus, who attracts all by His "unutterable beauty."[15]

III. We make contact with God where two or three are met
together in His name: in church, meditation, sacrament, the
preached word, worship and prayer.

IV. We approach God even as He draws near to us; for He
often comes, though sometimes in the disguise of those who love
and serve Him.

God for God's Sake

SCRIPTURE LESSON—ACTS 8:14-24, PHILLIPS.

Is our religion mostly magic or is it vitally Christian? In the interesting incident in our Scripture Lesson, this issue was sharply
drawn. Two men bearing the name of Simon fought verbally over
the question. When the man called Simon Magus (magician) saw
the power of the Holy Spirit mediated through Simon Peter, the
wonder-worker wanted it. He offered to pay good money for it.
Years later, heretics were called "simoniacs" after this mercenary

faker. Simon also gave his name to the sin of "simony," the use of money to attain spiritual ends.

Simon the magician keeps turning up in history. He lives among us now, and he lives in us frequently. He is the person who believes in God; he may even piously invoke Christ's name, and he works within the church; but he wants to use religion for his own or his group's benefit. Here the preacher may use a favorite illustration of current "simoniacs"—those who value religion for what it can bring by way of health, wealth and happiness. Consider how we have rediscovered God as a personal asset, and how we have wanted Him to produce tangible results for us. We go from the divine to the ridiculous. Apostolic scorn keeps scorching our superficial, self-centered distortions of the gospel. "When Simon saw how the Spirit was given through the Apostles' laying their hands upon people he offered them money with the words, 'Give me this power too. . . .'" But Peter said, "'To hell with you and your money! How dare you think you could buy the gift of God?'" Says Dr. J. B. Phillips in a footnote to this salty translation: "These words are exactly what the Greek means. It is a pity that their real meaning is obscured by modern slang usage."

Why this angry repudiation of Simon Magus and his brand of religion? Because God is not to be used. He is not a public utility in which we may be stockholders or directors. Here the preacher may well describe the Biblical portrait of the living God. The God of Israel, of the prophets, of the new covenant, the God and Father of our Lord Jesus Christ, is not to be tried and employed as we try or employ a vacuum cleaner, a dishwasher, or a garbage disposal. (See Isaiah 6; 43:1-3.)

Our God is: (A) our Creator and the Creator of all life, (B) the Lord of life who preserves and guides us, and (C) the God who redeems our souls from destruction at infinite cost to Himself.

59

You Can't Get These Pocket-Size

GOD IS INFINITELY GREATER THAN OUR HEARTS, AND HE
KNOWS EVERYTHING—I JOHN 3:20, PHILLIPS.

An article in *Changing Times* reads:

> Everything's getting smaller—at least in the wonder-world of
> electronics. Recent discoveries make possible palm-size TV cam-
> eras, wireless hearing aids the size of a nickel, and electronic
> computers not much bigger than a shoebox (some now require
> a whole room. . . . Batteries are also getting smaller. A nuclear-
> powered battery of miniscule size is said to be good for five
> years.

Everything getting smaller? Not in the field of the Spirit! Here
are certain realities and conditions which are not dwindling:

I. The human soul is not shriveling when it responds to the
divine Power which made it.

II. The human needs we should help God to meet are greater
than ever.

III. While God's greatness and knowledge may create fear and
even terror in some people, His love brings indescribable and
abiding comfort to those who have seen God in Christ, in Christ's
cross and resurrection, and in the continued ministry of the Holy
Spirit through the church.

60

How Simple Can You Get?

> BUT WE IMPART A SECRET AND HIDDEN WISDOM OF GOD,
> WHICH GOD DECREED BEFORE THE AGES FOR OUR GLORI-
> FICATION—I CORINTHIANS 2:7, RSV.

Distressed by the nonconformity of her son, an undergraduate in
his first course in philosophy, a mother said tearfully: "He's un-
willing to attend our church any more. He's arranged an appointment with a Unitarian minister because, he says, it's dishonest
for him to participate in a church service where the doctrine of
the Trinity is believed to be true." When I learned that the young

man was a neophyte in both philosophy and theology, and was "going steady" with a fine Unitarian girl, I assured the worried mother that her son might well think himself through to a more satisfying and mature religious faith. I realize that his difficulties might not be entirely intellectual.

But I was tempted to ask, with a smile of friendliness, "How simple can you get?" Why do you not discover for yourself why the church, through its intellectual and spiritual leaders, believed that the doctrine of the Trinity conserved profound truth concerning the nature of God? If you then reject the doctrine, at least you will realize that there is what Paul called "a secret and hidden wisdom of God," and a profound mystery surrounding the great Creator and Governor of the universe, the Lord of life.

I. Trust in God may seem to be simple, but the God in whom we trust is greater than we can imagine. William Beebe, the naturalist, told of visits he made to Sagamore Hill; he and Theodore Roosevelt would go out on the lawn at night and gaze up at the heavens to see who could first detect "the faint spot of light-mist beyond the lower left-hand corner of the Great Square of Pegasus." Then one or the other would recite:

> That is the Spiral Galaxy of Andromeda.
> It is as large as our Milky Way.
> It is one of a hundred million galaxies.
> It is 750,000 light-years away.
> It consists of one hundred billion suns,
>   each larger than our sun.

Beebe said that Mr. Roosevelt would grin at him and say, "Now I think we are small enough. Let's go to bed."[16]

Such perspective restores us to our proper place as little children, whatever our age or education. It may have been the attitude of Christians who asserted that to think of God too simply was unworthy and untrue.

II. We do well to reflect on the most unfathomable, mysterious doctrine of the church, the doctrine that God is Triune—three Persons in one Godhead. Too many of us who have real admiration and sympathy for what we call the Christian spirit, the Christian way of life, and the ethics of the Master, shy away from the creeds and doctrines of the church: "Why does the church take such a reactionary attitude? Why do Christian preachers sometimes say that what we believe matters greatly? Isn't it the kind of person I am that counts, and not whether I can dumbly assent to some complicated creed?"

It matters—what we believe about God. Remember that Jesus was crucified not for teaching love and kindness in human relations, basic as these are, but for blasphemy. He was slain for His unceasing loyalty to just those fundamental doctrines which the world condemns us for believing. The Trinity can never be adequately rationalized. "God" accurately defined would not be the great God whom we worship and adore. But to believe that God makes Himself known—and has within His being that which is expressed by Father-Creator, Son and Saviour, Holy Spirit, Life-Giver and Counselor—is much nearer to the truth about God than to think of Him as a vague, benevolent blur which somehow makes human hearts more tender and serene.

III. If you have a simple faith, keep it, live in it and by it; but do not dismiss as inconsequential the effort of the main body of the church to keep what seems to be, and indeed is, a highly complicated faith. It may be enough for you to sing "Jesus, Lover of My Soul,"[17] or "O Master, Let Me Walk With Thee,"[18] but without the church's insistence on the importance of creeds, you and I would cease to sing those hymns. Repeatedly, in history, when numbers of Christians abandon or minimize the classical beliefs of Christendom, the so-called simple gospel deteriorates and our faith becomes emasculated and weak.

61

What Can You Count On?

I AM THE LORD, I CHANGE NOT . . .—MALACHI 3:6, KJV.

"Never a dull lull" was a sign on a nightclub. It could be a sign over a church in some of our American communities. Life not only marches on, but goals are shifted and boundaries are changed. That which we thought permanent proves transient. Not only antiquarians, timid souls, and reactionaries, but every human being needs a certain amount of stability. Is there nothing that is changeless? Is there no fixed point of reference? Without change, growth would be impossible. This is a dynamic universe and God created it so. Nevertheless, what abides? "Chance and change are busy ever,"[19] says one hymn.

I. God is changeless in His essential being and character. Unlike His creatures, He is eternal. "They shall perish, but thou shalt endure . . ." (Psalm 102:26, KJV). Stars, planets, moons, earth, living creatures—everything—are in flux and know change. Here is truth on which to steady yourself when you feel that everything is spinning and the foundations are shaking ominously: God remains constant in His character. He is holy, righteous love. He is justice, beauty, goodness and truth. He who "so loved," centuries ago, continues to love today and forever.

II. God's purpose remains changeless. His grand design is to save us to a life of complete health and usefulness, of peace and joy. Is not this salvation? "He shall not fail nor be discouraged . . ." (Isaiah 42:4, KJV). Divine defeat is inconceivable. ". . . if we are faithless, he abideth faithful; he cannot deny himself" (II Timothy 2:13, ASV).

III. His promise never changes. Still, He says, in the words of a familiar hymn:

> The soul that on Jesus hath leaned for repose,
> I will not, I will not desert to its foes;
> That soul, though all hell should endeavor to shake,
> I'll never, no, never, no never forsake.[20]

Nor does His power diminish or change. David Livingstone said of Jesus that His is the promise of a gentleman who never broke His word.

IV. He who is changeless—from everlasting to everlasting, the same in power, wisdom, love and goodness—is yet the greatest source of beneficent change. Times and seasons, the course of events, evil men's designs, and best of all our human characters and lives, are changed by the One who abides our Saviour and our Friend.

Why Does the Church Exist?

SCRIPTURE LESSON—I CORINTHIANS 1:18-31, MOFFATT.

The church in Corinth faced real problems. Within its membership were critics, rebels and stand-patters. Factiousness, the curse of Greek political life, had penetrated the community of Christ and weakened the true power of the church. Paul himself had been severely criticized, and compared unfavorably with his colleague Apollos. He repudiated any basic difference between himself and his colleague and reaffirmed the gospel he had preached as the one wisdom of God. "God resolved to save believers by the 'sheer folly' of the Christian message" (v. 21). This folly is Christ crucified, the wisdom and power of God. This tremendous fact is the core of the Good News.

In the light of His guidance we may affirm reasons why the church exists:

To proclaim this Good News

To witness to God's mighty acts

To show forth the saving power of God in Jesus Christ.

There are other functions, as there are other services the church performs, but none are equal to these and none can be substituted for these purposes. Of course, the heralding—the witnessing—is accomplished through many media and instruments. Preaching, the sacraments, the realized fellowship, the intercessory prayers, and the outgoing service, are all means of proclamation. But service and mutual aid are not the reasons why the church exists. In the creative sense, the church exists to be Christ in the world. Christ is already in the world; we must testify, point to Him, make Him known, and show Him relevant.

What Kind of Church Do You Want?

CHRIST LOVED THE CHURCH AND GAVE HIMSELF UP FOR
HER, THAT HE MIGHT SANCTIFY HER, HAVING CLEANSED
HER BY THE WASHING OF WATER WITH THE WORD, THAT
HE MIGHT PRESENT THE CHURCH TO HIMSELF IN
SPLENDOR, WITHOUT SPOT OR WRINKLE OR ANY SUCH
THING, THAT SHE MIGHT BE HOLY AND WITHOUT BLEM-
ISH—EPHESIANS 5:25-27, RSV.

George Tyrrell said that at the end God will not ask what kind of
church you belonged to, but what kind of church did you long
for?

I. We long for a church that points away from herself to the
great God who made us and who loves us and who has redeemed
us.

II. We long for a church in which worship is given top priority;
worship as meaningful and God-centered as, with divine help,
we can make it.

III. We long for a church that will be inclusive in her fellowship, for in the presence of God, who made of one blood all men,
we are alike in origin and destiny, in need and longing.

IV. We long for a church that will live and die, like her Lord,
in the service of God.

Church: Organization or Organism?

SCRIPTURE LESSON—I PETER 2:10; I CORINTHIANS 12: 27; EPHESIANS 5:23, 29-30, RSV.

Is the church only "the religious arm of the community chest, or a Society for the Prevention of Cruelty to Human Beings," as Donald G. Miller satirically suggests? Is the Christian church, in any of its expressions, an association of "do-gooders," a mutual benefit society, or a kind of religious clinic for injured or sick souls? Is it primarily a fellowship of congenial persons interested in promoting helpful causes? It may be any of these, and yet it is more than all these put together. The church is both organization and living organism. The Bible gives the materials for this truth.

I. The New Testament concept of the church derives from the word *ecclesia,* meaning "the people who belong to the Lord." A form of this word appears 115 times in our New Testament. An *ecclesia* is more than an assembly of people. It is what the Old Testament means by "the Israel of God." God used the "old" Israel; when it became disobedient, God used the remnant of Israel still loyal to His Spirit and direction. Finally the choice narrowed. God sent His Son, Jesus the Christ. After Christ's death, resurrection, and ascension, God used His spiritual body, the church. That is why, in a profound sense, there is no such thing as a Christian apart from the church, which is the body of Christ.

II. The church is also described as "a temple of the Holy Spirit . . ." (I Corinthians 6:19, RSV). As the ancients met God in the temple, men and women now meet God in Christ, in the body of the living Lord.

III. A richly significant term for the church is "the body of Christ . . ." (I Corinthians 12:27, RSV). After Jesus left the sight of men, He returned in the Spirit to live in the church. "Wherever Jesus Christ is, there is the Catholic church."[21] Albert Schweitzer said that church members are part of the extended personality of Christ.

IV. A fourth figure for the church is "the bride" of Christ (Revelation 21, RSV). As the husband protects, cares for, and loves his bride, so Christ loves the church.

Like A Mighty Army

ONE IS YOUR LEADER, EVEN THE CHRIST—MATTHEW
23:10, MOFFATT.

From the memoirs of Field Marshal Bernard Montgomery comes
this sentence:

I had decided that in building up the Eighth Army for what
lay ahead [the campaign against Field Marshal Rommel, the
German military genius whom Montgomery ultimately defeated]
I would concentrate on three essentials: leadership, equipment,
and training.

Are not these also essential qualities for a successful church?
I. Leadership is given us in our living Lord, the Commander of
all the forces of goodness and redemption. Leadership among His
followers is found in those who serve.
II. Equipment is given by Christ: "His gifts were made that
Christians might be properly equipped for their service . . ."
(Ephesians 4:12, PHILLIPS).
III. Training for our long campaign in spiritual warfare is
provided by Him to whom the final victory belongs. "Can we not
much more readily submit to a Heavenly Father's discipline, and
learn how to live?" (Hebrews 12:9, PHILLIPS). (See also Hebrews
12:5 ff., PHILLIPS.)

In Spite of Everything

SCRIPTURE LESSON—HEBREWS 11:3-16, RSV.

When a person is reciting an experience, the phrase "in spite of everything" often occurs. In the letter to the Hebrews, the writer describes the pioneers who did not enter into the full heritage of faith. They were wanderers and nomads who never settled down. They were like so many of our junior executives and their families, forever moving on—sojourners and often strangers. Perhaps the ancient people felt, like the writer of Ecclesiasticus, wistful and uprooted. "Better is the life of a poor man under the shelter of his roof than sumptuous fare in another man's house." (29:22, RSV).

Christians are always en route, too. We are on a pilgrimage, and our home is forever beyond where we are now. Some reinforcing facts of the Christian pilgrimage can be gleaned from the Scripture Lesson.

I. In spite of everything, the pioneers in the Old Testament never lost their vision and their hope. They knew that it is better, as Robert Louis Stevenson affirmed, to travel hopefully than to arrive. What about us? Are we supported by the unfailing hope of Christ's promise?

II. In spite of everything, the Biblical wanderers never wished to go back. They seemed to know, as Thomas Wolfe's novel declares, that "you can't go home again," as far as an earthly shelter is concerned. Why do so many of us turn back so soon? Just around the corner may be our hearts' desire. Keep on keeping on, says the Scripture.

III. Those men were enabled to go on because they were haunted by the possibilities ahead. Travelers are haunted by thoughts of distant lands never seen. Artists, composers and writers are driven by what may be achieved. Said an old country farmer, "He who has something beyond need never weary."

IV. In spite of everything, God was not ashamed to be called their God. He loves the gallant soul who bets his whole life on God's Word. The man who plays it safe is not the person to whom the divine admiration is given. Because the old partriarchs were reaching out for something better, God was proud of them and prepared for them a city that has glorious and eternal foundations.

Young Church in Action

> THESE ARE THE MEN WHO HAVE TURNED THE WORLD
> UPSIDE DOWN. . . . SAYING THAT THERE IS ANOTHER
> KING CALLED JESUS!—ACTS 17:6-7, PHILLIPS.

Someone said that there are three classes of people: those who *make* things happen, those who *watch* things happen, and those who *have no idea* what is happening. A dynamic and devoted few in the early church were making things happen in the Roman Empire by initiating far-reaching changes, bringing to pass a new spiritual climate, and turning the world of accepted values and practices upside down because the wrong things were on top. To read and ponder the Acts of the Apostles is to know what was happening, who was making it happen, and how the twentieth-century church can become an equally vital, dynamic, and world-changing force. Dr. J. B. Phillips' title, *Young Church in Action*, aptly describes the New Testament community.

I. Who wrote the Acts? Luke, the beloved physician and author of the third gospel. When was it written? Probably about the year A.D. 85, although it is tempting to date it earlier, during the two years Luke waited with his chief, Paul, for the latter's trial in Rome.

II. What was Luke's purpose? To describe the march of the gospel and to show how the church grew numerically, geographically and spiritually. Acts 1:8 indicates the plan followed.

III. What was the message that shook the world? Read the first two Christian sermons in Acts 2 and 13. The basic affirmations are: (A) Jesus is the fulfillment of prophecy, and history's culmination; (B) the resurrection is everything: no resurrection of Christ —no church, no victory over death, and no conquest of this world; and (C) the gift of the Holy Spirit.

IV. What must be our response? We must examine our church to see if it marches in the apostolic succession and deserves apostolic success. The marks of the living church, which is ever renewing its youth, are: (A) dynamic inclusiveness; (B) militant action in winning recruits for Christ's active service force; (C) more consciousness of power than of problems, because an ever-living Lord through the indwelling Spirit nerves us for any campaign and any trial; (D) realization that our most formidable foes are enemies in our own household—the champions of the status quo and timid standpatters—who think that by opposing anything new they do God service; and (E) joyful, unconquerable courage.

68

Formula for Fellowship

I THEREFORE, A PRISONER FOR THE LORD, BEG YOU TO LEAD A LIFE WORTHY OF THE CALLING TO WHICH YOU HAVE BEEN CALLED, WITH ALL LOWLINESS AND MEEKNESS, WITH PATIENCE, FORBEARING ONE ANOTHER IN LOVE, EAGER TO MAINTAIN THE UNITY OF THE SPIRIT IN THE BOND OF PEACE—EPHESIANS 4:1-3, RSV.

How can we master the art of coexistence when we hold profoundly different convictions on so many issues? The disunity and discord in the world is a central thought in Ephesians, and it is the unshakable conviction of the author that in Christ all disunity and disharmony shall be resolved. All the barriers are to be destroyed because God's aim is what we call "a new togetherness." The church exists to transmit and apply this message, and Christ's love, to men everywhere. The church is intended to be an instrument to achieve true unity. To fulfill its high function, the church must have a certain kind of people. Paul, in Ephesians, tells us what kind of people we must be. William Barclay catalogs the qualities or virtues essential to the Christian in achieving with God "the new togetherness":[22] (A) Christian humility, derived from self-knowledge and from setting one's life beside the life of Christ; (B) gentleness, the spirit that is angry at the right time but never at the wrong time because it is God-controlled; (C) patience—the "long-suffering" of the old translation—the spiritually tough virtue that never gives in, refuses to fight back, and has the grace to endure insult and injury without bitterness; (D) Christian love—or *agape*, meaning "unconquerable benevolence"—which is more than an emotion or a sentiment; it is divine energy involving our wills; (E) peace—right relationships between men and women of different races, creeds, nations and classes—without which "men cannot be other than a disintegrated collection of individualistic and warring units," for disintegration follows after self-centered living.

At the masthead of the British weekly *The Christian World* was this motto: "In things essential, unity; in things doubtful, liberty; in all things, charity."

69

Three Chairs for Christians

AND WHEN THE HOUR CAME, HE SAT AT TABLE, AND THE
APOSTLES WITH HIM—LUKE 22:14, RSV.

One hundred and five years ago a book was published which said something significant concerning furniture. The book was *Walden* by Henry David Thoreau. The Yankee philosopher said that in his wilderness hut were three chairs: "one for solitude, two for friendship, three for society." Is any house or apartment complete without the spiritual equivalents of such chairs?

I. One chair for solitude symbolizes a continuing need of human beings in crowded cities, towns, suburbs and "exurbs." Professor Ashley Montague of Rutgers University has protested against the "annihilation of privacy." Roy Pearson jabs humorously at the multiplicity of meetings and other devices that destroy creative solitude:

All we wanted was the joy of not meeting—the privilege of silence, the right to be alone, the pleasure of staying at home with a book, the bliss of walking along a woodland path with someone beloved, the ecstasy of telling all the organizations of which we are members to hold as many monthly meetings as they wished, but not to save a place for us.[23]

Meetings can become "defense mechanisms which protect us from the need to inquire who we are and why we are here."[24] The Master loved people as persons. Because He had compassion for the multiude, He had to find solitude. Because He loved people, He had to leave people, regularly. He said, ". . . yet I am not alone, because the Father is with me" (John 16:32, kjv). "Come ye . . . into a desert place and rest a while . . ." (Mark 6:31, kjv), was His invitation to busy disciples. Is the Father of our spirits less real and intimate to us because we do not practice solitary meditation and communion? ". . . when you pray," He instructs us, "go into your room and shut the door and pray to your Father who is in secret; and your Father who sees in secret will reward you" (Matthew 6:6, rsv).

II. Two chairs for friendship. A person completely alone most of the time has difficulty being a real person. To live life to the full we need the sense of belonging to some of God's other children. We begin by becoming friends. If we draw a circle to shut any other out, because of his color, language, or cultural difference, we shut God out; and we shut ourselves out from enriching, humanizing and Christianizing experiences. Mature people have been marvelously described in Ephesians 2:19: "Now therefore ye are no more strangers and foreigners, but fellow citizens with the saints, and of the household of God" (kjv).

Centuries ago, when the saint named Columba established an outpost of the church on the famous island of Iona off the coast of Scotland, refugees began to come to the sacred isle to escape the violence of the warring clans on the mainland. Columba appointed monks to help the displaced, frightened and harassed exiles. He called the monks by a lovely name, "Soul Friends." The Bible advises us not to forsake our friends, but it also offers good news about God as the supreme Friend. Jesus said: "You are my friends if you do what I command you. . . . This is my commandment, that you love one another as I have loved you" (John 15:14, 12, rsv). He is the "Soul Friend" with whom any person may have intimate and deathless spiritual friendship.

III. Three chairs for society. This is where the church comes in. Rather, this is where we should come into the church—with our whole selves, all that we are and have. The Church is the divine-human society of believers in Christ. It is both world-wide and century-long in its fellowship. Someone jokingly asked a man in a tiny railroad station if he was in Grand Central Terminal. "No," the man replied, "but it's on the same line." Our church may not be the greatest in number, wealth, program or influence, but it's on the same line as the great church of the ages. Saints, apostles, martyrs, pioneers of faith, and benefactors of mankind are one with us in this redemptive community.

"Christ loved the church . . ." (Ephesians 5:25, RSV), says the New Testament. Because mobility marks our era, as no other has been marked, and because isolation makes fears and anxieties and sins harder to handle, we must learn to carry our burdens together. The cross of Christ is horizontal as well as perpendicular. The horizontal stands for our relationships one to another. God, who is symbolized by the vertical, intersects time and human situations to cleanse our horizontal relationships.

70

A Wall Is Something Between

FOR HE IS OUR PEACE, WHO HAS MADE US BOTH ONE, AND HAS BROKEN DOWN THE DIVIDING WALL OF HOSTILITY, BY ABOLISHING IN HIS FLESH THE LAW OF COMMANDMENTS AND ORDINANCES, THAT HE MIGHT CREATE IN HIMSELF ONE NEW MAN IN PLACE OF THE TWO, SO MAKING PEACE, AND MIGHT RECONCILE US BOTH TO GOD IN ONE BODY THROUGH THE CROSS, THEREBY BRINGING THE HOSTILITY TO AN END—EPHESIANS 2:14-16, RSV.

A weird advertisement appeared in a weekly small-town newspaper: "Christian wants the help of another Christian in erecting a fence." It may have been a legitimate request for help, but it looks suspiciously like a narrow, rigid religionist trying to find another with the same views. Fence building is never Christian work when it means erecting barriers between groups or between individuals. Paul's vivid picture is based on the series of courts, each one a little higher than the one before, that marked the temple plan. Between the Inner Court and the Court of the Gentiles was a marble balustrade. If a Gentile proceeded beyond it, into the Inner Court, he risked instant death.

I. One of life's tragedies is the wall we build with our prejudice, ignorance, unlovableness. Greeks called foreigners "barbarians," from "bar! bar!"—which was the way a foreign language sounded to them. A Dutch saying puts the truth succinctly: "Unknown makes unloved." Consider the danger of the zigzagging ideological fences that cross our planet today.

II. Bring Christ into an area of barriers and fences. He abolishes the separation because He is, as the Apostle affirmed, our peace. The surest way to achieve reconciliation between two quarreling persons is to bring in another whom they love and whose approval they value. The more people learn to love Christ, the more quickly they learn to love one another. Treaties, laws, leagues and societies may help, but they cannot bring lasting peace. Christ brings peace by making both Jew and Greek into new men. They become new in the sense that they become new kinds of persons. Christ does this by making them Christians.

III. Christ levels barriers between racial and religious groups by reconciling the opposing factions to God. "Reconcile," as used by Paul, means bringing together two friends who have been estranged. Each is given access to the one God and Father of us all. Such access and communion creates true community. Persons who are friends with God must be friends with each other.

Rita Snowden tells a World War II story: In France two soldiers and their sergeant took the body of a dead comrade to a cemetery for burial. A priest gently informed them that only Roman Catholics could be interred there, and they did not know what was their friend's religious allegiance. The priest said he was sorry, but he could not permit the soldier to be buried in ground his church regarded as consecrated. Sadly the G.I.'s dug a grave and buried their friend outside the cemetery fence. On the following day they returned to see whether the grave was all right. The priest told them that his heart had been troubled by his refusal to allow the dead soldier to be buried in God's acre. During the night he had risen from his bed, and with his own hands had moved the fence so that it might include the body of the soldier who had died for France and for human freedom. Love abolished the fence.

Jesus removes fences between man and man because He abolishes the kind of religion that is based solely on rules and legislation. He brings to men the true religion of love.

71

How Much Togetherness Can You Take?

AND AFTER HE HAD DISMISSED THE CROWDS, HE WENT UP INTO THE HILLS BY HIMSELF TO PRAY—MATTHEW 14:23, RSV.

"Togetherness" is a fairly new word describing an important condition of real living. "Community" is the term preferred by more serious writers, including theologians. As the essential gospel of Christ has been a major rediscovery of our time, so is the fact of the church as an integral part of the gospel and an indispensable part of salvation.

Togetherness destroys loneliness, the enemy of health and newness of life. Jesus selected the Twelve that they might be with Him. That was the divine method of training ambassadors of the Kingdom of God. It still is. Fellowship is one of the keys to the New Testament and Christian discipleship. Psalm 68:6 affirms a glorious fact of God's loving provision for our needs: "God setteth the solitary in families . . ." (KJV). We need each other. Individuals who pray—as well as work and play—together not only stay together for mutual strengthening, but achieve what no one member of the team may achieve.

Togetherness, at its Christian level, is essential to abundant living and to working with Christ for the realization of His design for men. In Paul's earliest writings he discussed its importance:

". . . comfort yourselves together . . ." (I Thessalonians 5:11, KJV).

But we can make a fetish and an idol of the concept. Charles Frankel of Columbia University recently made the churlish suggestion that

> Togetherness is becoming something of a nuisance. . . . One can detect the workings of the cult of togetherness, not only in family but in our approach to education, community affairs, business and politics, and in the longing which many of our most serious social thinkers permit themselves for other social orders more tightly knit than our own.[25]

"We need some separation to maintain a decent family," said the professor. Right! If sister had to play her records, if junior had to build his project, if father had to do his accounts or polish his woodwork, and if mother had to do whatever mothers have to do constantly—all at the same time and in the same place— families would be assaulted by more insidious things than secularism at its worst! Professor Frankel is sure that the word "together" raises three elementary questions: "Together with whom? Together for what purpose? Together how much?"

Repeatedly the gospels point out that Jesus found it necessary to withdraw from the crowd to clear His soul, to renew His physical energy, to recharge His emotional reserves, to make intimate contact with the Father. What about our church programs? Is it reactionary to ask ourselves searching questions about our efforts to get people together on committees, in groups, and in societies? Are we sometimes unconsciously undermining the very organism and institution we, as disciples, seek to promote, namely the Christian family and the Christian home? Togetherness may be so oppressive as to require participants to disengage themselves for the community's sake as well as for their own. Do we ever go up into the hills of vision and quietness to pray, to think and to "center down" in God? Unless we do, togetherness may become an enemy of Christian life.

How's Your Heart?

AND WHEN HE DEPARTED FROM THERE, HE MET JEHONA-
DAB, THE SON OF RECHAB COMING TO MEET HIM; AND
HE GREETED HIM, AND SAID TO HIM, "IS YOUR HEART
TRUE TO MY HEART AS MINE IS TO YOURS?" AND
JEHONADAB ANSWERED, "IT IS." JEHU SAID, "IF IT IS, GIVE
ME YOUR HAND"—II KINGS 10:15, RSV.

This quotation may sound like a solicitous friend asking a cardiac patient how he feels. Rather, it is the question a primitive warrior-king asked a prospective ally. Jehu was on his way to another massacre, but today we do not find his religious reasons convincing. "Zeal for the Lord" is scarcely justification for wholesale slaughter of enemies. John Wesley preached a famous sermon from this text, but he was careful to explain the context and to state clearly that he proposed to lift Jehu's question out of the setting in which it was asked. Wesley asked, What should a follower of Christ understand thereby when he proposes this question to any of his brethren? His sermon on "The Catholic Spirit" is an honest, searching answer.

Every day we confront the issue of Christian relations among men and women and children of different racial backgrounds. To examine the issue with a minimum of emotion is an obligation for all who follow Christ, and for all who love their country and desire that it should be truly Christian.

I. Agreement on basic matters—faith in God, love of Christ, desire to see His kingly rule of righteous, holy love prevail in every area of human activity—can be reached among persons of diverse background, color, social and economic status. Without oversimplifying the problem or its solution, is not the essential thing the One who unites us?

> Not what I do believe
> But Whom! . . .[26]

II. When essential agreement is discovered, hearts beat in the same rhythm of understanding and Christian love. "Is your heart as my heart?. . . .Give me your hand." Differences and doubts on secondary matters may remain, and Christians continue to differ on many creedal and liturgical points, but the more Christ's love permeates our lives, the more we can unite on things that matter most.

III. Only as Christ lives in our hearts can our hearts be right and our hands joined in brotherly affection and co-operation. "For this reason I bow my knees before the Father, from whom every family in heaven and on earth is named, that . . . he may grant you to be strengthened with might through his Spirit in the inner man, and that Christ may dwell in your hearts through faith . . ." (Ephesians 3:14-17, RSV). "Here"—the Apostle writes of the heart, the inner life and spirit—"there cannot be Greek and Jew, circumcised and uncircumcised, barbarian, Scythian, slave, free man, but Christ is all, and in all" (Colossians 3:11, RSV).

73

Making a Marriage Christian

MAKE LOVE YOUR AIM, AND EARNESTLY DESIRE THE
SPIRITUAL GIFTS . . .—I CORINTHIANS 14:1, RSV.

Marriages are made neither in heaven nor in Hollywood, although heaven can exert a good influence on an earthly marriage. A Christian approach contributes to a Christian achievement. F. Townley Lord lists four suggestions for happy Christian marriages:

I. Work at your partnership.

II. Married love lasts when we remember such simple things as anniversaries, courtesies, appreciations and continuing courtship.

III. Your heart is where your treasure is.

IV. A mind sharing is a mind strengthened.

How to Get More out of the Bible

AND SO WE ARE CONTINUALLY THANKFUL THAT WHEN YOU HEARD US PREACH THE WORD OF GOD YOU ACCEPTED IT, NOT AS A MERE HUMAN MESSAGE, BUT AS IT REALLY IS, GOD'S WORD, A POWER IN THE LIVES OF YOU WHO BELIEVE—I THESSALONIANS 2:13, PHILLIPS.

Who reads the Bible? Not a fraction of the people who praise it as the greatest of all classics. Few homes are without a copy of the volume praised as the "Book of books," and every hotel and motel makes it available. Is the Bible opened by those who see it? Some twenty-three million copies are distributed each year throughout the world, but almost every week a clergyman, teacher, judge or social worker complains that the persons with whom he deals never open a Bible. William Neil has said, "We have the curious paradox of a Book that is still accepted as an integral part of the life of society, but largely disregarded; a world best-seller that nobody seems to read." Who reads the Bible? Preachers? Sunday school teachers? Simple natives in the "younger churches"?

Why isn't the Bible read by more intelligent persons today? Because for many its authority has been undermined by science. Some people feel that the space age has made the world of the Bible seem foreign, remote and unreal; yet human nature and its elemental needs remain essentially unchanged. To these deep needs the Word of God coming through the Bible speaks as no other word can speak.

How can we get more out of Bible reading?

I. Obtain a copy which is readable. Many translations are available now. One of the modern translations may overcome much of the antipathy for an "antique book."

II. See the Bible for what it is: not a textbook on science or ancient history, but the unique record of God's search for man and man's response to God. It is, as Professor Neil writes, an interpretation of life and an invitation to creative living. It interprets the universe to us: it shows us who we are, where we came from, why we are here, and what may be our destiny. Supremely, the Bible interprets the ultimate Reality to us: the nature and purpose of God.

III. The Bible, transmitting the living Word of God, challenges us to decision. Will we decide for or against the life that is life indeed: the life in Christ, in the community of God's people? Will we accept the liberation won for us, offered to us, in the Lord Jesus Christ? We have not as much faith in the Bible as we have faith or trust in the God whom the Bible reveals. Christ is the center and goal of Scripture.

75

A Bible Bouquet of Sweet Peas

SCRIPTURE LESSON—PSALM 23, KJV.

I. *Possession*: "The Lord is my shepherd. . . ." In each of the six verses of this psalm there are one or more personal pronouns. There are seventeen in all.

II. *Position*: "He maketh me to lie down in green pastures. . . ." A believer in God's universe knows satisfaction and rest.

III. *Pardon*: "He restoreth my soul. . . ." "Restoration" means "realized forgiveness." A new start and a new life are possible to the one who has been cleansed, healed, and restored to the Father's family.

IV. *Progress*: "Yea, though I walk through the valley of the shadow of death. . . ." Says one preacher: "The spiritual poet compresses into this verse the great fundamentals: light, life, fellowship and progress. God rewards faithfulness with spiritual development. We are traveling on. We will walk *through* the dark valley."

V. *Provision*: "Thou preparest a table before me in the presence of mine enemies. . . ." Enemies may be fear, anxiety, loneliness, bereavement, materialistic concepts of success, and doubt. Strength and encouragement are provided by our bountiful God in the midst of opposition. The manna falls in the valley through which we move.

VI. *Prospect:* "Surely goodness and mercy shall follow me all the days of my life: and I will dwell in the house of the Lord for ever." "Follow" means "pursue." God in Christ is indeed "the Hound of heaven," following us with love and mercy. In a life lived in Christ the words of a serialized story are always true: "To be continued. . . ."

76

God Breaks Through the Death Barrier

> BUT GOD RAISED HIM UP, HAVING LOOSED THE PANGS
> OF DEATH, BECAUSE IT WAS NOT POSSIBLE FOR HIM
> TO BE HELD BY IT—ACTS 2:24, RSV.

At the Langley Field Air Force Base in Virginia, some new jet planes were making a spectacular series of flights. As they whined, roared and boomed at undisclosed speeds, an Air Force officer tried to enlighten me: "Every plane you have seen can break the sound barrier. Our next job is to invent a plane and equip men to break through the thermal barrier—the heat barrier. Once we do that, landings on other planets and return flights will be nearer realization."

Will man ever break through the final barrier—death? For the Christian there is incontrovertible evidence that one Man broke through the death barrier and lives to prove it. The Man is Jesus Christ. Declared the Apostle Peter, on the famous day of Pentecost, "This Jesus God raised up, and of that we all are witnesses" (Acts 2:32, RSV).

Consider then the *fact* and the *force* of God, in Christ, breaking through the death barrier:

I. The Book of Acts stresses the resurrection as final proof that Jesus was indeed God's chosen One. New Testament scholars remind us that Acts is the "Gospel of the Resurrection." How often it has been said from the pulpit, and rightly, that without Christ's resurrection there would have been no Christian church. Theologians and Biblical scholars agree that the early preaching made the resurrection central and basic to the Good News.

Is the resurrection historical? Is it truth through parable? Is it a myth, in the deepest meaning of "myth"? Increasingly the weight of evidence confirms the New Testament claim that Christ rose from the dead and that the empty tomb attested to a true resurrection; it was not a revival of One who had not actually died, or the spiriting away of the body of Jesus who subsequently lived only spiritually in the hearts of His followers. This does not mean that we are concerned about whether or not the physical body of Christ was reassembled. Indeed, St. Paul declares, ". . . . flesh and blood cannot inherit the kingdom of God, nor does the perishable inherit the imperishable" (I Corinthians 15:50, RSV). We believe in the resurrection of Christ's "body"— all that identified Him to those who knew Him in the days of His flesh. We realize that in a profound sense the church, the redeemed and redeeming community animated by His Spirit, is His body in the world now. But Christ's personality survived physical death. ". . . it was not possible that he should be holden of it [death]" (Acts 2:24, KJV). Can you conceive of personality without some kind of body? Our Christian conviction is far different from and far more than the old Greek or even the modern concept of absorption of the human spirit into some vague deity.

II. Christ's breaking through the death barrier, and all other evil which sought to annihilate Him, is a fact. From it there issues a tremendous *force*, a power by which we can live and conquer our own enemies. This is the power of truth over falsehood, of goodness over evil, of life over death, and of love over hatred. The risen Lord breaks through every barrier of death.

Eschatology for Moderns

> THEN COMES THE END, WHEN HE DELIVERS THE KING-
> DOM TO GOD THE FATHER. . . . THE LAST ENEMY TO BE
> DESTROYED IS DEATH. . . . THE STING OF DEATH IS SIN.
> . . . BUT THANKS BE TO GOD, WHO GIVES US THE VICTORY
> THROUGH OUR LORD JESUS CHRIST—I CORINTHIANS 15:
> 24, 26, 56, RSV.

I. Death, "The last enemy to be destroyed . . . ," must be shattered if God's will for His human creatures is ever to be realized.

II. Christ draws the sting from death by enabling us to lose self-love in the love of God in Christ.

III. Resurrection is God's act, and it is God's gift to all who commit themselves to Him.

IV. We have power here and now to live by the resurrection faith.

III

CHRISTIAN ANTIDOTE FOR CRISIS

Conversation at Midnight

... ABOUT MIDNIGHT PAUL AND SILAS WERE PRAYING
AND SINGING HYMNS TO GOD, AND THE PRISONERS WERE
LISTENING TO THEM, AND SUDDENLY THERE WAS A
GREAT EARTHQUAKE, SO THAT THE FOUNDATIONS OF
THE PRISON WERE SHAKEN; AND IMMEDIATELY ALL
THE DOORS WERE OPENED AND EVERY ONE'S FETTERS
WERE UNFASTENED—ACTS 16:25-26, RSV.

At midnight—in prison. Can you picture a darker situation for
good men? It could be the time when the butterfly of panic
emerges from the chrysalis of fear, but not for the two valiant
souls described in this chapter. ". . . at midnight," as the King
James Version puts it, "Paul and Silas prayed, and sang praises
unto God. . . ."

I. We may be in the midnight of our era. We are living with
ugly facts that will not vanish: irresponsibility and corruption
among "power groups," high and low; the Communists' success
in technological and scientific fields where we thought we were
unbeatable; the fear of war and the ever-present blight of sin in
our souls. It is more than Shakespeare's "winter of our discontent."
At midnight—war and rumors of war. At midnight—man lost in
the darkness of his own follies. At midnight—Is our only conversation one of despair and foreboding? No. Like Paul and Silas,
today's Christian knows of another and divine factor.

II. At midnight Paul and Silas prayed and sang hymns to God.
They did more than whistle in the dark to keep up their courage.
They knew the worst, but they knew One who could use even the
worst for the best purpose. When you know who is coming to
the world, and who is in control, as we Christians know, then
there are gleams in the darkness which point to conflict and to
God's victory.

A Christian view of history shows that the prison doors to the
human spirit can be swung open. In the religious outlook, all is
not superficially bright or irremediably dark. Granted, there is

too much use of religion as a kind of tranquilizing drug or a public utility. But there are the facts of the World Council of Churches, the manifest concern that our unity in Christ must be realized and expressed more dynamically, and the evangelistic enterprise. Individuals are being transformed through encounters with the living God in Christ. We know, as the disciples before us knew, that "the church is an anvil which has worn out many hammers."[1] Therefore, however dark the outlook, we know that immeasurable cosmic forces are at work and that these forces are destructive only to self-satisfaction and corruption.

III. At midnight we Christians must rally the frightened and depressed souls around us. The jailer would have committed suicide had it not been for the swift and heartening word from Paul. Midnight is an excellent hour in which to communicate the Good News.

Long ago a saintly French woman named Madame Guyon spent ten years in prison, and during that time she wrote this song:

> Nought have I else to do,
>   I sing the whole day long;
> And He whom most I love to please,
>   Doth listen to my song. . . .
> My cage confines me round;
> Abroad I cannot fly;
> But though my wing is closely bound,
>   My heart's at liberty.
> My prison walls cannot control
> The flight, the freedom of the soul.[2]

In such confidence we find the triumph of Christian experience, and this experience "worketh . . . hope" (Romans 5:3-4, KJV). We are servants of the One who is able to open prison doors and unfasten fetters. Into suffering and evil, as well as into the hidden heart of God, Jesus our Lord flashes His light.

IV. We can do more than encourage and inspirit fearful and discouraged men and women around us. At midnight we can give them the Good News of release from every bondage. Modern men and women may not ask, as did the jailer of the Apostles, "What must I do to be saved?" But if we listen for the cry beneath whatever words may be used, we know the ancient question is still being asked. The glorious Good News is still "Believe in the Lord Jesus, and you will be saved, you and your household" (Acts 16:31, RSV). We know One who said, "I am the door . . ."

(John 10:7, KJV). Of Jesus Christ alone can it be said, "He who has the Son has life. . . ." (I John 5:12, RSV). When the disturbed jailer trusted the Lord, who was commended to him by two of His representatives, he was "baptized at once, with all his family" (Acts 16:33, RSV). More than this, he ministered to them, "brought them up into his house, and set food before them . . ." (v. 34, RSV).

Is it midnight in your world? Do you feel shaken to the depths by earthquake experiences? You too can rejoice, with all your household, that you believe in God.

79

Swaying Pillars

> AND SAMSON GRASPED THE TWO MIDDLE PILLARS UPON WHICH THE HOUSE RESTED, AND HE LEANED HIS WEIGHT UPON THEM, HIS RIGHT HAND ON THE ONE AND HIS LEFT HAND ON THE OTHER. AND SAMSON SAID, "LET ME DIE WITH THE PHILISTINES." THEN HE BOWED WITH ALL HIS MIGHT; AND THE HOUSE FELL UPON THE LORDS AND UPON ALL THE PEOPLE THAT WERE IN IT—JUDGES 16: 29-30, RSV.

Is there an analogy in the destructive power of the sightless giant, not unvisited by gleams of divine grace, chosen because of his tremendous strength to be an instrument for the fulfillment of a divine plan?

I. Is militant Communism such a giant? Will Marxism, in its Stalin or Khrushchev versions and combined with Russian imperialism, bring the house of modern civilization crashing about our heads, or those of our children? Is it not true that the immense technological skill and manpower of such nations as Russia and China could be capable of shaking the temples of our way of life? Some former Communists insist that the West, and all lovers of human dignity and freedom and spiritual faith, cannot do business with this giant. But we must live together in the same world, or not live at all.

II. Is secularism such a giant? Secularism is life without God, and secularized human beings have their temples and their equivalent of the pagan deity Dagon. How lightly we take the demands of true religion. Yet how cleverly and masterfully we have created a giant, an electronically-operated donor of much that pleases. But suppose the giant itself and our trust in it bring down the temple of life?

III. The things that are shaken, both Old and New Testament Scriptures insist, are shaken that the things which are true and enduring may be revealed. The impact of forces hostile to Christianity and to responsible democracy may benefit us immensely. The giant who shakes us may force us to examine the foundations on which our lives rest.

Recall the story of Winchester Cathedral in England. It had been built over a bog, on a foundation of tree trunks laid on top of the watery soil. As the cathedral walls began to settle, they cracked. Then the engineers dug down through eight feet of wet peat and built a new and solid foundation.

How is the foundation of our social structure? Have we built Christian truth into the basic element? Have we strengthened the fabric with Christian faith? Or are we resting on pillars of paganism? ". . . if the foundations are destroyed, what can the righteous do?" (Psalm 11:3, RSV).

IV. The psalmist gives materials for the answer: ". . . the Lord's throne is in heaven. . . . he loves righteous deeds; the upright shall behold his face" (vv. 4, 7, RSV). Thus, when the pillars seem to shake, undergird your soul with the "foundational" truths of the Bible: (A) God is just; the Bible's word is righteous. (B) God is love; this is the Good News of Christ. Therefore (C) God has the last word, and the last word is that good is victorious over evil. God cannot be sabotaged by the wickedness of men. God reigns. God loves. God controls. And when the columns of man's temple begin to sway, we must lead our brothers—blinded giants or overwhelmed pygmies—to "the rock that is higher than I" (Psalm 61:2, RSV).

He's Got the Whole World in His Hands

IN HIS HAND ARE THE DEEP PLACES OF THE EARTH: THE
STRENGTH OF THE HILLS IS HIS ALSO—PSALM 95:4, KJV.

AND I GIVE UNTO THEM ETERNAL LIFE; AND THEY SHALL
NEVER PERISH, NEITHER SHALL ANY MAN PLUCK THEM
OUT OF MY HAND. MY FATHER, WHICH GAVE THEM ME,
IS GREATER THAN ALL; AND NO MAN IS ABLE TO PLUCK
THEM OUT OF MY FATHER'S HAND—JOHN 10:28-29,
KJV.

If you ever fly in a plane and encounter turbulence of a severe
nature, you should repeat these affirmations to yourself. You
might even hum the haunting lyrics of the spiritual:

> He's got the whole world in His hands;
> He's got the big, roun' world in His hands;
> He's got the wide world in His hands;
> He's got the whole world in His hands.

See also Psalm 139: "Even there shall thy hand lead me, and thy
right hand shall hold me" (v. 10, KJV).

I. Spiritual security is bestowed by Christ upon every one who
hides his inner life with Him in God (Colossians 3:3).

II. Our divided world can be held together only by men and
women of every race and nation who are united in Christ. Only
God, who makes Himself vividly and redemptively known in Jesus
Christ, can convince us that we are "no more strangers and foreigners, but fellowcitizens with the saints, and of the household
of God" (Ephesians 2:19, KJV). F. Scott Fitzgerald left a plot idea
for a novel based on an estranged family who inherited a grand
house and estate which they could claim only if they succeeded in
living together amicably in the house. What about this house of
our world?

III. This world of God's and man's has much grim evil in it.

But God, not evil, has the last word. "... the whole world lieth in wickedness" (I John 5:19, KJV), but the power of wickedness is within the controlling power of God.

IV. If these things are true, then we must join God in recovering this planet for Himself. Missions are therefore imperative. If Christianity is not good enough for Russia, Korea, Japan, China and Africa, it is not good enough for America. If Christianity is not good enough for the slum areas, it is not good enough for the Fifth Avenues and the Park Avenues. God has the whole world in His hands. In a profound sense, also, He has no hands but our hands to do His work today.

81

Dependables in a Tumbleweed Culture

> I KNOW THE ONE IN WHOM I HAVE PLACED MY CONFIDENCE, AND I AM PERFECTLY CERTAIN THAT THE WORK HE HAS COMMITTED TO ME IS SAFE IN HIS HANDS UNTIL THAT DAY—II TIMOTHY 1:12, PHILLIPS.

> SINCE THEN WE HAVE BEEN GIVEN A KINGDOM THAT IS "UNSHAKABLE", LET US SERVE GOD WITH THANKFULNESS IN THE WAYS WHICH PLEASE HIM . . .—HEBREWS 12:28, PHILLIPS.

What are the dependables we can count on through personal relationships and through experimentation?

I. God, with whom there is no variableness.

II. Jesus Christ, who is the same yesterday, today and forever, and who demonstrates the reality and love of God.

III. God's Kingdom, or fatherly rule, among men and nations.

IV. Love, which is greater than faith and hope, and particularly that Love which will not let us go.

V. God's saving community, the church of Jesus Christ, against which even the gates of hell and the forces of evil shall not prevail.

What Hope for a Better World?

IN OUR MOMENTS OF IMPATIENCE LET US REMEMBER
THAT HOPE ALWAYS MEANS WAITING FOR SOMETHING
THAT WE HAVEN'T YET GOT—ROMANS 8:24, PHILLIPS.

I. Christians are neither shallow optimists nor unrelieved pessimists. We acknowledge the element that William James called "real wrongness in the world." Wrote a theologian,

> God has undertaken to carry out His purpose with us in a
> world of uncertainty, because only a world of uncertainty is a
> world of possibility, and only a world of possibility contains the
> conditions of mortal growth.

God has a goal that He has unveiled in Christ and through Christ. He summons us to work with Him for its attainment.

II. We hope persistently, not only because we see signs of Christ's growing triumph, but because God is the infinite Factor in every equation and situation. Evil can and does delay the ultimate victory, but the end is sure. For us, as for Paul, life need not therefore be a despairing waiting period before inevitable defeat, decay and death. Life is an eager anticipation of a liberation, a renovation and a re-creation worked by the power of a glorious God.

Wanted: A New Imperialism

THE KINGDOM OF THE WORLD HAS BECOME THE KING-
DOM OF OUR LORD AND OF HIS CHRIST, AND HE SHALL
REIGN FOR EVER AND EVER—REVELATION 11:15, RSV.

Imperialism is an ugly word in most circles today, and rightly so, for it connotes domination of the weak by the strong. But, more than ever, a spiritual imperialism is imperative. Why?

I. All nations need Christ.

II. Every human being needs Christ's remedy, the gospel, and the gospel must be adapted to every human being.

III. Christ and His truth are the great uniting powers that will bring nations into harmony and mutual trust.

IV. If Christ's empire must be universal, then we must be His agents, His transmitters and His ambassadors.

84

A Word for the Human Race

> BUT SEEK FIRST HIS KINGDOM AND HIS RIGHTEOUSNESS,
> AND ALL THESE THINGS SHALL BE YOURS AS WELL—
> MATTHEW 6:33, RSV.

In an editorial in *The New York Times*, an informed political thinker, and an essentially Christian one, pleaded for "a patriotism of humanity." Surely this is close to what our Lord meant when He urged His followers to seek first God's Kingdom and His righteousness. Whatever eschatological meanings may have been in Jesus' mind, the immediate, this-worldly application cannot be denied.

Are there measures which "little people" like ourselves may take to create, widen and implement "a patriotism of humanity"? A statesman has listed three essentials of Christian civilization:

I. *Peace*. No one wants to fight under modern conditions of warfare. No civilized order for mankind can be achieved and maintained in a state of war "from here on out."

II. *Freedom*. This is essential to building a Christian community of persons or of nations. We must join others everywhere who will work for peace and the removal of any threat of war. We must also extend true freedom, and resist any attempt in the name of "realistic politics" or "ecclesiastical policy" to curtail the freedoms already won.

III. *Law.* The rule of law is necessary because freedom and peace are meaningless unless guaranteed by law. Christian freedom is "ordered" freedom. Christians insist that citizens be responsible citizens.

Where do Christ and religion enter into our consideration of these essentials? In everything. Harold A. Bosley has quoted George Washington's belief that this nation, "kept consciously under God, can achieve a much higher form of democracy than history has any record of, up to date." In his farewell address, Washington urged his fellow countrymen to attend constantly to the worship of God. "Can it be," he asked, "that Providence has not connected the permanent felicity of a nation with its virtue?" What is true for our nation must be true for all nations, for "God so loved the world." Through Christ we must love the world in such fashion and spirit that impediments to God's design may be removed.

85

Look in the Rearview Mirror

> ... IF ANY ONE IS A HEARER OF THE WORD AND NOT A DOER, HE IS LIKE A MAN WHO OBSERVES HIS NATURAL FACE IN A MIRROR; FOR HE OBSERVES HIMSELF AND GOES AWAY AND AT ONCE FORGETS WHAT HE WAS LIKE. BUT HE WHO LOOKS INTO THE PERFECT LAW, THE LAW OF LIBERTY, AND PERSEVERES, BEING NO HEARER THAT FORGETS BUT A DOER THAT ACTS, HE SHALL BE BLESSED IN HIS DOING—JAMES 1:23-25, RSV.

To look in the rearview mirror frequently as you drive is essential to safe driving. To look in the rearview mirror of history—personal, national, human, and what theologians call "sacred history"—is essential to salvation and great living.

I. Look in the rearview mirror along the highways of life in order to see that much of the past was far from good, and that God has dealt radically and transformingly with it.

II. Look in the rearview mirror of Biblical faith in order to see how God has dealt with our sorry past. ". . . he has visited and redeemed his people . . ." (Luke 1:68, RSV).

III. Look in the rearview mirror, and by using the insight of the Apostle James, learn to drive on the King's highway with attention to what matters.

86

Greet the Unknown with a Cheer!

> . . . HE KNOWETH WHAT IS IN THE DARKNESS, AND THE LIGHT DWELLETH WITH HIM—DANIEL 2:22, KJV.

Psychologists say much about what lies hidden in the darkness of our minds. Dreams give clues to things buried deep in our unconscious. Not only in our spiritual darkness, but at every step of the way in life, mystery confronts us. Daniel thanked God for giving light to interpret what was in the darkness.

I. Our ignorance of the future should inspire us to thank God and take courage. In His valedictory, Jesus told His disciples that they were to be left to face the future without His visible presence. "I have yet many things to say to you, but you cannot bear them now" (John 16:12, RSV). If you and I were sure of serene days ahead, we would grow slack, lazy and complacent. Conversely, if we were clairvoyant and could discern a series of black tomorrows, with illness, accidents and death coming to us or those we love, we would be utterly despairing and depressed.

II. Relief and encouragement come when we rest our minds in the thought that God knows what lies ahead and that He is the Christlike Father. " . . . he knoweth what is in the darkness. . . ." He is not an abstraction or a nebulous force; He is much more than a mathematical mind raised to the infinite power. He is the God and Father of our Lord Jesus Christ. His name is Love.

III. Greet the unknown future with a cheer because the tomorrows belong to God, as do the yesterdays and todays. Pierce Harris once said, "The man who keeps one eye on the past and one eye on the future will be cockeyed in the present!" But the man who keeps his eye on God's loving wisdom and unfailing presence will be able for anything. Whatever we must face tomorrow, God will be in it too. Hugh Redwood remembers a time when he was troubled about a decision. He was shown into a quiet room, and on a table near the fireplace he saw an open Bible. He read these words: "The God of my mercy shall prevent me." "Prevent" is an old English word that means "go before." Someone had written another rendering in the margin: "My God in His loving kindness shall meet me at every corner." If we walk with Him, we walk in the light. Trust where you do not see: ". . . he knoweth what is in the darkness, and the light dwelleth with him."

87

Living Toward the Future

> . . . WHO HAVE TASTED THE HEAVENLY GIFT, AND HAVE
> BECOME PARTAKERS OF THE HOLY SPIRIT, AND HAVE
> TASTED THE GOODNESS OF THE WORD OF GOD AND THE
> POWERS OF THE AGE TO COME . . .—HEBREWS 6:4-5,
> RSV.

If any generation ever tasted the powers of the age to come, it is our own. Lunar thrusts, intercontinental guided missiles, satellites in orbit, jet planes and electronics—these are a few listings in the catalog of tomorrow's world which are being realized today. But if we have atomic power and no other power, we shall be, of all creatures, those most swiftly liquidated. We must taste "the heavenly gift" of God's grace; we must become "partakers of the Holy Spirit" and know what it is to taste "the goodness of the word of

God." The dynamics of contemporary science must be matched and molded by the dynamics of Christ's gospel in our personal and social lives.

I. Christ, risen and abiding in His church, gives us power to work for the kind of life we would like to see in the ages to come. ". . . to all who . . . believed in his name [in His nature and in His spirit], he gave power to become children of God . . ." (John 1:12, RSV). To as many as link their lives with His life today, through trust and obedient response, He provides spiritual resources to work for a humane and Christian community for all His children.

II. Christ, alive in and with His own in His body—the church, the company of believers, and the community of the redeemed who are committed to be redemptive—can help us as persons to live toward the future with confidence and joy.

"To live toward the future" sounds like a New Testament phrase. It has New Testament truth in it. It comes, however, from one of the most unusual novels of our time, *Doctor Zhivago*. Before you read more than ten pages, one of the characters, Nikolai Nikolaivich, says:

> History as we know it began with Christ and that Christ's Gospel is its foundation. . . . It was not until after the coming of Christ that time and man could breathe freely. It was not until after Him that men began to live toward the future. Man does not die in the ditch like a dog—but at home in history, while the work toward the conquest of death is in full swing; he dies sharing in this work.[3]

CHRISTIAN CALENDAR

Sunday Miracle

I WAS IN THE SPIRIT ON THE LORD'S DAY—REVELA-
TION 1:10, RSV.

"A miracle in a prison camp, and on a Sunday?" To many good citizens, who can either take their church on Sunday or leave it alone, this event seems incredible. Of course, they say, Sunday is a wonderful day, particularly if it means a day of rest and recreation, with a party or a game to relieve the lulls. But a miracle on Sunday?

In your imagination, paint the picture of John sitting by the seashore, perhaps after a restless night, turning in thought toward Jerusalem, thinking of the little church at worship lifting him up to God with their intercessions. Then hear the cries of sea birds, the roar or moan of the waves breaking on the island's coast, the whistling winds merging with the vision granted him. Like Isaiah, John sees the Lord on high and lifted up. He is in what we call a trance, but his experience is authentic. He sees that the Being whose majestic appearance and character he tries so hard to describe is the A to Z of real life, the Alpha and Omega. And John is never the same again.

I. The worship of God in Christ in church can work this miracle for us. Divested of the imagery and external features of John's vision, the encounter is still possible. We draw near to God in our prayers and praises, and in all that we mean by corporate worship, and we find Him drawing near to us. He sets before us the quest that disturbs us, and makes Himself known to cleanse, to heal, to renew and commission. Our appointment at church on Sunday is an invitation to experience the miracle of contact with the eternal God.

II. In our Christian worship another mysterious, tremendous miracle is possible—the miracle of a changed life and a renewed mind. This is what a great preacher described in his sermon, "Miracles of Character Possible to All." Not only to the elected and selected great, but to ordinary people Christ comes in His Spirit, saying, "Come after me and I will make you. . . ." Again and again this has happened, not always in formal church services, but in church more often than many suppose. Wilfred Grenfell, a young medical student, drops in at a church service where the American evangelist, Dwight L. Moody, is preaching. The young man experiences a profound change of mind and soul, and becomes a great medical missionary to neglected Labrador fishermen and their families. A chronic alcoholic comes to church with a friend. Both men are skeptical of the therapeutic effect of this visit, and both men are given a "jolt" out of their skepticism and habitual way of living. Within a few years they become dependable, outgoing, happy Christian workers. How often has the Lord fulfilled His promise to meet with two or three who assemble in His name and in faith!

III. On Sunday, in the company of other worshipers of God, we may help God work the miracle of banishing loneliness for those who feel strange and foreign, unknown and unloved. It is in fellowship, animated and controlled by love of God and man, and inspired by the Holy Spirit, that togetherness becomes real. As all human minds may be united at a very deep level, so when human minds unite in prayer, God releases power, love and acceptance from one mind to and through another. "No man is an island"; worship in church helps a man to realize his oneness with God and with his neighbor. This transformation of life and direction, this vision of the living God, this replacement of loneliness by companionship at its best—"This is the Lord's doing; it is marvellous in our eyes" (Psalm 118:23, KJV).

89

12/20/64

How Christ Comes to Us Today (*Advent*)

FOR WHERE TWO OR THREE ARE GATHERED IN MY NAME, THERE AM I IN THE MIDST OF THEM—MATTHEW 18:20, RSV.

SO HE WENT IN TO STAY WITH THEM. WHEN HE WAS
AT TABLE WITH THEM, HE TOOK THE BREAD AND
BLESSED, AND BROKE IT, AND GAVE IT TO THEM. AND
THEIR EYES WERE OPENED AND THEY RECOGNIZED HIM;
AND HE VANISHED OUT OF THEIR SIGHT—LUKE 24:29-31,
RSV.

. . . LO, I AM WITH YOU ALWAYS—MATTHEW 28-20, RSV.

During a period of fierce opposition to organized religion in So-
viet Russia, the secret police raided a humble home where they
knew a Christian group met for study and worship. After identifying the offenders, the officer in charge announced that there
were seven under arrest. "No," corrected an aged Christian, "there
are not seven, but eight." Annoyed, the officer counted again.
"Seven is all I find," he said. "Who is the eighth?" "Jesus our Lord,"
came the response.

Many noncommunists might agree with the Russian officer that
the old believer who made the declaration of faith was naïve, if
not superstitious. Certainly many of us would say that such belief
implies a mystical attitude we do not possess. Nevertheless, Scripture and the experience of nineteen centuries support the man's
claim. Jesus Christ is risen, therefore alive, therefore available to
all who put their trust in Him and seek to obey His spirit. However we may explain the Holy Spirit, it is part of His work to make
Christ real, to bring His teaching to our attention and understanding, and to kindle in our inner lives, as in the corporate life of the
believing community, the light of His presence.

How does Christ come to us now?

I. Christ comes wherever His followers meet together to worship God in His faith, name and love. Charles B. Williams has
translated Matthew 18:20 in this manner: "For wherever two or
three have met as my disciples, I am right there with them." Do
we come to church expecting this appointment to be kept?

II. Our Lord manifests Himself to those engaged in Christlike
action on behalf of any of his children, anywhere. The testimony
of the mechanic in Sir Ernest Shackleton's Antarctic expedition
across polar wastes could be made in many different situations:
"Boss, I had a feeling there was not just three of us, but four." This

surely is part of the teaching of Jesus' own parable of the last judgment: ". . . as you did it to one of the least of these my brethren, you did it to me" (Matthew 25:40, RSV). He was present in the person whose needs were met. Can we explain the early church's phenomenal expansion in any way other than the power Paul referred to when he was among hostile forces: "The Lord stood by me"?

III. Christ comes in every circumstance and in any location: ". . . lo, I am with you always." He reveals Himself to those who trust and obey Him as He cannot reveal Himself to others. Reflect on the slang phrase "Get with it," or "Get with him." We may be alongside a person in a meeting and not be "with" him. Or, we may be thousands of miles from a loved one and yet be closer to that person than to someone in the same room with us.

IV. Christ comes to us in a specific manner through the sacrament of the Lord's Supper. It is indeed Holy Communion. It is not only the memorial He "hath willed us to make," not only the celebration of the covenant or agreement He has made, and not only the giving or renewing of our vow of loyalty to our divine Lord and Leader; it is contact with Him in a spiritual relationship. Theologians have agreed on this basic matter. They differ, often profoundly and bitterly, in the manner of His coming. Donald M. Baillie said that God knew we needed not only the Word made flesh; but after the flesh had vanished, we needed the Word made sacrament.[1] It is neither Word nor sacrament that saves us, but God Himself. Yet God uses both Word and sacrament. Baillie adds: "Christ is as truly present to the faith of the receiver as the bread and wine are to his outward senses."

90

Christ Comes Again (*Advent*)

THEN HE RETURNED FROM THE REGION OF TYRE, AND WENT THROUGH SIDON TO THE SEA OF GALILEE, THROUGH THE REGION OF THE DECAPOLIS—MARK 7:31, RSV.

Jesus was rejected by the Gadarenes, and He is rejected by many of us. We reject Him when we refuse to let Him determine our stand on vital questions and conduct. When we send Him away, does He go forever? An old Scottish saint named McCheyne said that Christ has the last as well as the first knock on the door of human lives. Is this true? Certainly it seems that Jesus decided a second visit to the Nazarenes would do more harm than good. But His attitude toward Gadara was different. Rejected and spurned by them, He came again.

In this season of Advent the church stresses the second advent, the return of Christ to the world that so largely rejected Him when He first came. We celebrate the glorious truth that Christ comes again. Whether or not He will return visibly and physically, as many devout Christians firmly believe, Christ comes again in the mysterious power and reality of the Spirit.

I. He comes a second time, and a third, and only God knows how many more times, even when we reject Him and His claim on us. We send Him away, only to realize that without His love and truth our burdens become insupportable, and life is dreary if not disastrous.

II. He comes again to our society even though it has spurned His wisdom about life. Robert Menzies has written:

> Does this age, with its chaotic morality, its supression of human freedom and threat of atomic war, support the optimism of the social meliorists? Life itself is taking up the challenge, and reducing to absurdity man's baseless belief in his capacity to achieve personal and social salvation. Our Lord Christ's time is coming. He is the only One who can afford to wait. And when our age has drunk the last draught from the bitter waters of experience, He will come again, this time not to be cast out but welcomed as Saviour.[2]

III. Christ comes again in every personality which willingly becomes the instrument of His love. A missionary in the Manchurian hinterland told his audience about Jesus, etching with words the portrait of Christ. When he finished, they said, almost unanimously and with smiles of appreciation, "We know this Jesus. He has lived among us." They took the missionary to the grave of a Dr. Jackson. In this faithful follower of Christ, who went about doing good, the people had discerned Dr. Jackson's Lord. "So long as the church can produce saints, the gates of hell will not prevail against it," said William R. Inge. You and I may add,

"So long as the church produces Christlike men and women and boys and girls, Christ comes again in power."

IV. Has Christ come for you and to you? Christmas is coming, but

> If He's not born in thee
> Thy soul is still forlorn.[3]

A. J. Ebbutt has written:

> There are many Second Advents. Jesus came only once in the flesh; he comes a second time as a spiritual Presence. . . . The living hope we cherish, imbedded in the doctrine of Jesus' Second Coming, is that the final victory is with God.[4]

91

Ready for Christmas? (*Christmas*)

COME; FOR ALL IS NOW READY—LUKE 14:17, RSV.

Even efficient persons can omit something from the Christmas list. But Christmas is much more than preparing gifts. It is a time to receive God's unsurpassed gift of Himself in the Son of His love. Are you ready to receive?

I. If you could have asked this question of men in the old Roman Empire into which Christ came, you would have received two apparently contradictory answers, each containing incontrovertible truth: (A) that the world of the first Christmas was ready, for the preparatory work seemed complete and the psychological moment had been reached, and (B) that a majority of individuals —Herod, among others—were not ready for the revelation of Christ.

II. Is our world ready for Christmas and ready to welcome Christ to His rightful place as Lord of life and Determiner of destiny? Our very fears and anxieties, our unquenchable longing for something—for Someone—to give our lives meaning, completion, and true security, prepare the way for Christ's coming. Being ready for Christmas means house cleaning, sweeping out the moth-eaten beliefs, rusty prejudices, soiled and useless habits.

92

Watch for This Sign (*Christmas*)

> AND THIS WILL BE A SIGN FOR YOU: YOU WILL FIND A BABE WRAPPED IN SWADDLING CLOTHS AND LYING IN A MANGER—LUKE 2:12, RSV.

I. Follow the sign to the manger, and it shall lead you to a revolutionary concept of man's true status.

II. Follow the sign, for it signifies that the mighty God, the everlasting One, has come down to us where we are and where we live in our need and longing.

III. Follow the sign, and you shall discover that God's concept of power is our idea of weakness.

IV. Follow the sign to Bethlehem, to Galilee, to Calvary and Olivet, if you would know that life which ultimately is victorious.

93

God Has Come! (*Christmas*)

> SCRIPTURE LESSON—ZECHARIAH 2:10-13, KJV.

How perfectly the Messianic prophecy was fulfilled in Jesus Christ! Think of the declaration in I John 5:20 (KJV): ". . . we know that the Son of God is come. . . ." The New English Bible translation reads: "We know that the Son of God has come and given us understanding to know him who is real; indeed we are in him who is real, since we are in his Son Jesus Christ."

I. Christmas is the celebration of many things. Supremely, it celebrates the birth of a Child, over nineteen hundred years ago, in a village now located in the Kingdom of Jordan. The child was named Jesus, and He became a Man. We Christians have learned to speak of Him as Christ, the Messiah, the uniquely commissioned One who represents and demonstrates God. When we say that He is our Lord Jesus Christ, we affirm that He is the unique expression of God in history; and that as God has been eternal, so Jesus Christ was and remains. He is the personification of the divine Reality at the heart of all existence. God has come! You have seen advertisements for stereophonic phonographs and recordings. Surface noise is almost eliminated, say the manufacturers and salespeople. The sound that is reproduced is so natural that as you listen you may have almost the same experience as you would have sitting in a concert hall where the artists were playing. Jesus, born of Mary in Bethlehem over nineteen centuries ago, is the truth and love and wisdom of God recorded with the highest fidelity possible on a human instrument. "God was in Christ . . ." (II Corinthians 5:19, RSV), said Paul, one of Christ's ablest interpreters and most ardent followers. God is in every human being, says the prologue to the Gospel of John. But always there have been imperfections, "surface noises" in the other human instruments. In Jesus, all the fullness of the Godhead, all the divinity which could be contained in a human personality, was present.

How do we know? How can we say, with the Prophet John, ". . . we know that the Son of God has come . . ." (I John 5:20, RSV)?

II. To quote the Scripture, Jesus Christ has "given us understanding, to know him who is true" (I John 5:20, RSV). To use another word in place of "understanding," Christ has given us discernment to come to know the Real One. When we read the New Testament we are conscious of the fact that when Jesus speaks, God is somehow speaking; when Jesus heals, God is healing; when Jesus forgives a sinner, it is God forgiving a sinner; when Jesus gives up His life on Calvary's cross, somehow God is on the cross, too. As we enter the spiritual presence of Christ, God comes near. The Incarnation is God speaking in words we can understand, acting in ways we can grasp, taking shorter steps so that we can keep up with Him.

III. ". . . we know that the Son of God has come . . ." because the world is different since He came. A victory has been won, in advance, over the forces of evil. True, it often seems, as the New Testament writer said, that "the whole world is in the power of the evil one" (I John 5:19, RSV), with wrong upon the throne. But through the eyes of our faith we know that God has landed on our planet, that the Deliverer has arrived, and a death blow has been dealt to our greatest enemy. In the words of an unknown poet:

> Now a new power has come to the earth,
> A match for the armies of hell.

". . . we see not yet all things put under him. But we see Jesus . . ." (Hebrews 2:8-9, KJV). Dark and menacing is the outlook in our world, but God in Christ is at work. We need to remember not only what might come to the world, but who has come to the world. Something in the coming of Jesus changes the whole situation. New powers for transforming evil into good have been released. This is a redeemed world because Christ has claimed this earth for His own, and we can trust Him to make good His claim.

IV. ". . . we know that the Son of God has come . . ." because when we are "in Christ"—united to Him through our trust and love and obedience, and united with Him through membership in His body, the church—we have power to live victoriously. "The Lord sets the prisoners free . . ." (Psalm 146:7, RSV). A famous British prime minister, William Ewart Gladstone, said, "One example is worth a thousand arguments." It is true. When a person goes out to do what others talk and argue about, he furnishes the most convincing argument of all. Jesus Christ lived the life, and He left us an example that we should follow. But an example alone would leave us defeated. We live by the grace of the Son of God who loved us and gave Himself for us. This was the refrain of the early church. Today, it is the testimony of countless men and women who are masters of circumstance, of temptation, of failure, of fear, "through Jesus Christ our Lord." As John wrote, "We know that no child of God is a sinner; it is the Son of God who keeps him safe, and the evil one cannot touch him" (I John 5:18, NEB). Evil cannot really touch him in such a way as to wound him mortally, or throw him, or start the disease of sin raging through him again. As one Christian thinker phrased it, "A child of God may sin, but his normal condition is resistance to evil." We certainly have an active enemy, but thanks to God

for His gift of Christ, we also have a watchful and invincible De-
fender. A saint is a Christian who may fall now and then, but who
gets up again and keeps on trying to live the life he has glimpsed
in Christ.

V. ". . . we know that the Son of God has come . . ." because,
through out commitment to the God he reveals, we have "life
plus," or what the Bible calls "eternal life." It is more than ever-
lastingness or a shadowy continued existence. We have life with
the deepest dimension; life abundant, purposeful, exhilarating,
which marches through bodily death into that which we cannot
picture. "This is the true God and eternal life" (I John 5:20, RSV).
Do you recall reading, perhaps telling, the lovely story of the
English postal clerk who handled letters that went into the dead-
letter section because they could not be delivered? The man had
lost his little four-year-old son and he was deeply depressed. One
letter he picked up was addressed to Santa Claus and it was written by his seven-year-old daughter, Ann. After telling Santa that
Christmas was not going to be very happy in her home, she asked
him to help her family. "Could you stop by and pick up Eddie's
little wagon and take it to him. He loves it so, you know. And then
about Daddy, Santa—I heard him say the other day that nothing
but eternity could ever make him feel better. Santa, I don't know
what eternity is, but if you have any of that, will you please bring
some to my Daddy to make him smile again. Lovingly, Ann."

". . . he has put eternity into man's mind . . ." (Ecclesiastes 3:11,
RSV). He brings eternity to us, by transforming our transient existence into life plus, into life eternal. In His unique redemptive
power, God has come to us intimately and wonderfully. "Joy to
the world, the Lord has come!" "O come, let us adore him, Christ
the Lord."

94

Wrap It Up (*Christmas*)

SO THE EXPRESSION OF GOD BECAME A HUMAN BEING
AND LIVED AMONG US. WE SAW HIS SPLENDOR . . .—
JOHN 1:14, PHILLIPS.

Christmas shopping brings to salespeople the frequent request, "Wrap it up." Modern advertising refers to a deal, a commodity, or a television program as being "packaged." Men and women adept at expressing ideas are hailed for their ability to "wrap things up neatly." Occasionally we say, "Wrap it up," when we mean "Make it final."

In every culture of which records have survived, men and women believed in some kind of supernatural power. God-seeking, and occasionally God-finding, marks primitive and civilized peoples alike. Among the world's sacred literature the Old Testament stands supreme in testifying to God's self-revelation of His nature and intentions to a community with a peculiar genius for religion.

Prophets and saints knew God to be perfect in wisdom, power, holiness and righteousness. The most perceptive and advanced among them believed that His mercy and love were complete and beyond anything the most loving human parents could possess and show. But abstractions were not enough. Even visitations by God's Spirit seemed to bring less than absolute satisfaction.

I. We need peace of soul. Much can be done to acquire it through study of books and through examination and practice of basic principles. But only when peace is "wrapped up" in a peacemaking person do we really grasp it. ". . . . he is our peace . . ." (Ephesians 2:14, KJV). God wrapped up his idea of peace in One who came not only to divide the good from the evil, but also to give His deep, unbreakable peace to all who trust in Him. In Christ we see the conditions whereby we may have peace even in the midst of inevitable conflict.

II. We need forgiveness and acceptance. When we read how others have received it, we realize that true forgiveness comes wrapped up in a person. When someone we have wronged says— without treating the wrong lightly—"I forgive you," then we experience pardon. The fact of God's forgiving love was known by believers before Jesus of Nazareth was born in Bethlehem, but only since Jesus lived and died, breathing forgiveness toward His crucifiers, have we understood what it means and costs. When in Christ's spiritual presence we confess our sins, repent of our wrongness, and trust Him for forgiveness, we know ourselves to be forgiven and restored to the family.

III. We need power to live unselfishly every day. Abstract principles help—a little. But only when we tap resources of strength in a personal way do we feel adequate. "I can do all things in him who strengthens me," is Paul's testimony (Philippians 4:13, RSV). Countless others have verified that truth in their experience of Christ. Jesus is all of God that could be projected into a single human personality. He is all we need to be strengthened with might by God's Spirit within us. Moreover, seeing Him do the work of a servant makes it possible for us, in our pride, to humble ourselves.

IV. We need God. Love divine and eternal, love redemptive and death-conquering—only as we behold these tremendous "ideas" wrapped up in the life and Spirit of God's Son, can we make contact with God.

V. God still needs us to wrap up His ideas and hopes for mankind. As Rita F. Snowden said, it is "without doubt, the second great wonder in the world" that God still desires to wrap up His ideas in persons—in you and me. The Incarnation must continue through us, for God's sake and the world's.

95

How Much? (Lent)

> FOR THE SON OF MAN . . . CAME NOT TO BE SERVED BUT TO SERVE, AND TO GIVE HIS LIFE AS A RANSOM FOR MANY—MARK 10:45, RSV.

Rita F. Snowden recalls reading in an early travel book about Russia that an English-speaking traveler was able to find his way through the vast country by mastering two simple Russian words. One was the word for tea and the other was the word *skolko*, meaning "How much?" When he needed food, lodging, transport or clothing, he asked, "*Skolko?*"

Lent should be a season in which we take a serious look at interior discipline. We should grow in grace by our concern for skill in prayer, worship, Bible interpretation and application, and in winning others to Christ and the church. How much do we really want? How much are we prepared to pay?

I. One way to deal with the cost of Christian living would be to face the question, How much have we been given? Said Albert Schweitzer:

> One thing stirs me when I look back at my youthful days—the fact that so many people gave me something or were something to me without knowing it. . . . Hence I always think that we live, spiritually, by what others have given to us in the significant hours of our life. . . . Out of the depths of my feeling of happiness, there grew up gradually within me an understanding of the saying of Jesus, that we must not treat our lives as being for ourselves alone.[5]

II. How much do we have that we did not earn or deserve? Life, love, friendship, freedom, our country, our health, and what Ian Maclaren called "the kindly light of reason"? Our salvation? How much shall we give in return? The tag end of our days, the last frayed ounce of our energy? The "tips" of our income? A novelist said:

> I ask that I may be permitted to love much, to serve to the utmost limit of my capacity, and to keep faith with that high vision which men call God. I shan't do it wholly. Nobody does that. I only want never to stop caring.

How much will you give in exchange for a life forgiven, transformed and made thrilling with meaning and hope in Christ? How much will you give to make the Lenten season an enriching, growing time for your fellow souls?

96

Why Did Jesus Die? (Lent)

FOR THE LOVE OF CHRIST CONTROLS US, BECAUSE WE ARE CONVINCED THAT ONE HAS DIED FOR ALL; THERE-FORE ALL HAVE DIED. AND HE DIED FOR ALL, THAT THOSE WHO LIVE MIGHT LIVE NO LONGER FOR THEM-SELVES BUT FOR HIM WHO FOR THEIR SAKE DIED AND WAS RAISED—II CORINTHIANS 5:14-15, RSV.

Our predecessors in the Christian faith spoke much of Christ's atonement. Sometimes they spoke in terms that seem to us almost blasphemous. Legalistic theories almost blotted out the love of God operating in the life and death and victory of Jesus. Historical theology bears scars of battles over the attempts to enforce one theory upon another. But historical theology also confirms our own "educated guess"; namely, that in Christ's death on Calvary's cross, something cosmic, something of immeasurable power for human beings, was done which man could not do for himself and which need never be done again.

In looking again at this mystery of the cross, we may follow the late Donald M. Baillie's outline of a sermon on the question, "Why did Jesus die?" His text was Romans 5:8. Dr. Baillie dealt with the question in its most profound meaning. He asked, "What is the ultimate meaning of the crucifixion of Jesus in the eternal counsel and purpose of God?" His outline was based on three questions, "leading on from the simplest to the deepest":

I. "Why did they get Him put to death?" Because the religious leaders of the Hebrews were shocked by Jesus' attitude toward sinners. He was more interested in black sheep than in any other kind. Publicans, prostitutes and profiteers were among His hosts and friends. But even worse, Jesus lumped the respectable—the "unco' guid," of whom Robert Burns wrote scathingly—with the dregs of society. All had sinned, Jesus implied.

II. "Why did Jesus Himself choose to die?" He could have escaped such a bloody end. He could have evaded His enemies and cheated them of their satisfaction. But to escape would have been to abandon His mission, and that would have meant abandoning God's children. As theologians insist, endorsing the New Testament claim, there is a "plain, historical and local sense" in which He died for sinners. Why did He choose to die? Because He loved sinners with a love that would not let them go.

III. "What was the meaning of the death of Jesus in the eternal purpose of God?" As the witnesses of His death thought about it, they became convinced that Jesus' self-sacrifice had something to do with the love of God, the Creator of the universe, the Source of all life, the Architect of every living creature's destiny, the Father of human spirits. Instead of losing faith in God's love, as we might have expected them to do, they were convinced by the Man on the central cross of God's undying love. God demonstrated His love for us, said Paul to the Christians in Rome, in that while we were yet sinners, Christ died for us. In our text, "he died for all, that those who live might live no longer for themselves but for him who for their sake died and was raised." He died that He might bring us to God as restored, forgiven, accepted children of our loving, heavenly Father. These early Christians were sure that God must be like Jesus, going to infinite lengths to assure us of His love, achieving oneness with us and we with Him.

Dr. Baillie summarized memorably:

> That is why Jesus died. With all the other answers that we give, we can't stop short of that deepest of all answers. Jesus died on the Cross because it was God's will to come right into our sinful, fallen situation, and, incarnate in a man, to bear upon himself the sin of the world.

What must we do because of this love—this dying and undying love—for us, for all men?

97

Victory Parade (*Palm Sunday*)

SCRIPTURE LESSON—THE GOSPEL NARRATIVES OF THE TRIUMPHAL ENTRY.

I. This was a strange victory parade, for only the Leader of the procession understood its meaning.

II. This parade and its sequel in the upper room were planned by Jesus.

III. This parade into His nation's capitol was an exhibition of Jesus' sublime courage.

IV. This parade represents Jesus' claim to be King.

V. This parade was Jesus' last appeal to the citizens to accept Him as their true Lord and King.

Miracle in Three Acts (*Easter*)

SCRIPTURE LESSON—LUKE 24: 15-53, RSV.

Ernest Trice Thompson, in his discussion of the Easter narrative in Luke's final chapter, concentrates on the three parts of the day which shook the earth and still shakes it—the day of Christ's resurrection.[6] Said a former editor of *Time* magazine, "There has been no new news on either subject [life or death] for some time—nearly two thousand years in fact. The resurrection was tremendous good news, if true." He remarked that in spite of the Christian communication of nearly twenty centuries, the resurrection of Jesus is widely disbelieved. "Live yourself into his story and see whether it is true," we need to tell ourselves and our listeners. We have had detailed reconstructions of the day Christ died. But look at the day Christ was raised from the dead, to die no more.

I. Morning (Luke 24:1-12). All New Testament accounts of the resurrection begin with the discovery of the empty tomb at dawn. Women first made the discovery. Their report to the disciples seemed incredible and was discredited. Those in the inner circle of Jesus' first followers were not looking for anything more than a kind of vague immortality. Have we considered that the Easter truth has triumphed in spite of resistance by men in every age (see John 20:8)?

II. Afternoon (Luke 24:13-31). Two men were trudging along the road to Emmaus as the twilight descended, and a third man joined them. Was there ever a more surprising journey, a more startling conversation, a more divine Guest welcomed to supper? In this section you may deal with the fact that the two pilgrims were confused by the events of the weekend. "... we had hoped ..." (v. 21, RSV). But hope died on Friday. Then Jesus opened to them the Scriptures and the faith that releases hope. Easter was the day on which hope was born again. As He broke the bread in that dearly remembered way He had done it before His death, their eyes were opened. They knew that Jesus—crucified, dead, buried

—was alive! He was their Guest and Host, and the Companion of their days forever.

III. Evening (Luke 24:33-43). Although the two disciples undoubtedly had planned to spend the night in Emmaus, the disclosure of the risen Lord made them scrap that idea. They rushed back to the city to share the marvelous news with their colleagues. They found the others, except Thomas, huddled in the same meeting place where they had shared a last supper with Jesus before His ugly death. Before the Emmaus travelers could utter a syllable, they were told that the Master had appeared to Peter. Then they poured out their story. As they did, the Lord Himself suddenly appeared in the room. The accounts indicate that His manifestation evoked fear, dread, terror. The disciples thought He was a ghost. Jesus convinced them that is was He, but they continued to doubt, as when joy surprises us we find it hard at first to believe.

Have you read about the hunted Jewish refugees who hid underneath Cologne Cathedral during the Nazi terror? Written on the walls of their secret refuge were these words: "I believe in the dawn, even though it be dark; I believe in God, even though He be silent." This is the Easter conviction. This is what we learn when we "live ourselves into the story" and find our hearts warmed by His invisible presence.

99

4/14/63

Who Meets the Risen Lord Today? (*Easter*)

SCRIPTURE LESSON—MATTHEW 28:8-10, NEB.

This is the day above all days for Christians, for this is the anniversary of the day the living Christ overcame death. To the risen Lord the church owes its beginning, and to the everliving Lord the church everywhere owes its existence, its confidence, its power, and its hope. A devout and learned scholar said recently that for the Christian the resurrection of Jesus is not so much an event in history—even the greatest event in history—as it is "a reality which must be appropriated." One way to appropriate this reality is to ask to whom the risen Christ appeared. Then we shall have a key to the question, To whom does He make Himself known as the living Christ today?

I. Christ appeared, after His death on Calvary, to one who loved Him. In the center of every picture of the resurrection is one person: Mary Magdalene (Matthew 27:56, Mark 15:40, John 19:25, Matthew 27:61, Mark 15:47, Matthew 28:1, Mark 16:1, Luke 24:10, John 20:1). She owed everything to Jesus, and she knew it. Is it not significant and hopeful that Jesus appeared in His risen glory to one whose only claim was that she loved Him?

II. Christ appeared to a man who was genuinely sorry because he had denied the Highest. It does seem that the second appearance of the risen Master was to Peter (Luke 24:34, I Corinthians 15:5; see also Mark 16:7). Could any man be more heartbroken and ashamed than the Big Fisherman after he had denied his Lord? A lesser man would not have been with his colleagues when Jesus returned from death. Why did Jesus want Peter to know that He was alive and with him? Surely, to save Peter from destructive self-contempt and self-hatred. Does it not lift our own spirits to know that Jesus makes a personal visit to the life that is truly penitent and desperately in need of God's forgiveness?

III. Christ appeared to bewildered and discouraged travelers who longed for some light of meaning in their darkened lives. To the two journeying to Emmaus, He appeared when they were trying to find some explanation of the tragedy they had witnessed (Luke 24:14-21). Somehow this crucified Galilean Master had remained at the heart of their shattered world. It still happens. Problems are immense and darkness does envelop our minds; mystery is an impenetrable curtain. But if Jesus and His claims are kept in our remembrance, He draws near and light shines in the darkness. Then we go on our way, attended by a Presence unseen and real.

IV. Christ came through the gates of death and through the door of a barricaded room to where men were almost faint with fear. He appeared to His followers in the upper room, when they were shaken by the events of Calvary. They had reached the depths of despair, and there they found God. Even in their fear, Jesus was the Center of their thinking. Christ still comes to those who follow Him, at least with their minds, despite their anxiety and fear.

V. The risen Lord appeared in a special way to a man who was filled with doubt. Thomas' doubt was a brittle, intellectual skepticism. It was truly an agony. He needed desperately to believe, but his belief required the consent of his rational nature. Let a person ask honest questions, present honest doubts, and keep struggling for assurance, and the risen Lord will return to him.

VI. The risen Christ made Himself known to two desperate men who had fought a kind of battle against Him. Jesus appeared to James, one of His brothers who had not believed in him (John 7:5, I Corinthians 15:7). He appeared also to Paul (I Corinthians 15:8; Acts 9:1-9, 22:1-11, 26:1-18). Both men took Christ seriously enough to oppose Him. They were neither indifferent nor neutral. If a person takes Christ seriously enough to oppose Him, Christ has a way of confronting him, often winning an advocate from the very person who was an antagonist.

VII. Last of all, the risen Christ manifested Himself to the church. It was a pitiful little remnant, yet in that group of followers who met together we have the nucleus of the holy catholic, or universal, church. Is there any place where Christ makes Himself more vividly and transformingly known than where men and women and boys and girls assemble for prayer, praise and worship in His name and faith?

On Easter, and on all tomorrows, the risen Lord makes Himself known to the bewildered seekers of reality; to the fear-haunted who still keep Him at the center of their minds and emotions; to the honest doubter who keeps his mind open to the possible disclosure of truth; to the person who takes Christ seriously enough to try to refute and oppose Him; and to His own people when they meet together in the mysterious engagement we call worship.

100

The Glory of Now (*Easter*)

BUT NOW IS CHRIST RISEN FROM THE DEAD—I CORINTHIANS 15:20, KJV.

The words "but now" are freighted with meaning. Consider three of Christ's transformations that are registered by the words "but now."

I. Christ alive in our world, through the power of the Holy Spirit, changes isolated, individualistic and lonely persons into members of the divine community.

II. Christ, risen and victorious, abiding in and among His people—the church—changes darkness into light for all who confide in Him and with His help follow Him.

III. Christ, by His resurrection, completely and gloriously changes the human situation.

101

Through the Barricade of Death (*Easter*)

SCRIPTURE LESSON—I CORINTHIANS 15.

For the Christian, Easter is the affirmation that death's barricade has been forever shattered by life. It has been said that death guards its secrets well, and this very secretiveness frightens and dismays many persons. At least, the complete lack of communication from travelers to that undiscovered country fills many with doubt. Notwithstanding many cogent arguments by philosophers for personal survival of physical death, there is no conclusive assurance of it, apart from Christ's revelation of God's love and His own resurrection from the dead. But we have Christ's assurance, both verbal and actual. As the Apostle Paul declared in his letter to the Corinthian colony of Christians: "Christ died, . . . he was buried, . . . he was raised on the third day, . . . he appeared to Cephas, then to the twelve. Then he appeared to more than five hundred brethren at one time, most of whom are still alive, though some have fallen asleep" (vv. 3-6, RSV). This the church affirms. Moreover, the church could cite an innumerable company of other witnesses to Christ's resurrection. They may not have seen Christ with their physical eyes, but they have seen Him with faith's vision. He has made Himself known to them in the breaking of bread, in the taking of the cup of fellowship, in their championship of His cause, and in their service of His Kingdom.

What of us on the anniversary of His resurrection? Do we have the certainty of Paul and the early church? Christ breaks through the barricade of our doubt and unbelief if we can say with Paul, "Last of all, . . . he appeared also to me" (v. 8, RSV).

I. It is only when the Lord appears to me and you that the resurrection becomes a reality for us. The other appearances are important; this personal encounter is decisive. Only this personal revelation enabled Paul to speak of "the power of his resurrection . . ." (Philippians 3:10, RSV). Not argument, nor impressive evidence furnished by others, but a great love had taken possession of his life.

II. A great love from a living Lord and Friend can change lives. Silas Marner was transformed by the love of a little child. In one of her *Sonnets From the Portuguese,* Elizabeth Barrett Browning said that the face of all the world was changed for her by Robert's love. To Paul, the love of Christ was a soul-shaking experience. Think how life moved into depths and breadths and heights undreamed of when a similar love grasped Francis of Assisi, Mary Slessor, Albert Schweitzer, or Toyohiko Kagawa. It is when you and I can say, not only "He is risen," but "He appeared to me," that something happens.

III. How can the Easter fact and the love of Christ become a living power in our lives? It will not come by mystic vision, nor will we gain it by acknowledging ourselves to be Christians. A spiritual leader of our time suggests that the barricade will be breached by God in Christ if we meet certain practical demands. (A) We must place ourselves in the way of receiving. We must live as if He is alive. This means that in our relationships with others, in business deals and in everyday actions, we must act as if He is present. We must wish to choose as He would wish. (B) If He is alive and near in the world of spirit, He is near enough for us to communicate with Him. This means we must rediscover the meaning of prayer. We must take time to establish contact with His living Spirit and find regular times for prayer and meditation —at least a weekly appointment in the place where, with "two or three," He will keep His promise to be present. These are simple demands, but meeting them will lead us into an ever-deepening experience of His presence and power. Not by any emotional "rock-and-roll," but by consequences in life, we shall be able to say, "Last of all, . . . he appeared also to me."

Why the Resurrection? (*Easter*)

SCRIPTURE LESSON—COLOSSIANS 2:11-12; 3:1-5, 12-17.

Christian teaching clearly indicates that eternal life is not an inevitable sequence to this earthly existence, nor is resurrection unconditional for every human being.

I. Spiritual surgery by the divine Physician Jesus Christ makes a man ready for life, here and hereafter. Christ alone can cut away from a man's personality everything that handicaps him and prevents him from being God's obedient child. Paul says that this very act took place in our Christian baptism. In the early church, baptism meant that a definite and life-changing decision had been reached. It was adult baptism, it was instructed baptism, and it was baptism by immersion. Therefore the symbolism of this sacrament or ordinance was easily understood. As the baptized person rose from the water, he symbolized a man rising to life anew. But this symbolic resurrection took place only when the individual trusted in the divine love and power operating through the life, death and resurrection of Jesus Christ. If God could raise Christ from the dead, He could raise the trusting believer also.

II. Colossians 3:1-4 clarifies "the power of the resurrection" here and now. The risen life is a different life.

(A) The Christian's thought-life is directed toward those things that have an endless future. He sets his heart on "things that are above. . . ." Everything in this world is seen against the background of eternity. This gives the Christian a new set of values; a new way of judging persons, events, things; a new sense of proportion. How does this happen? As a dead body is hidden in the earth —the Greeks spoke of burial in this way—so a personality given newness of life is hidden in Christ, or wrapped around with Christ.

(B) Christ Himself becomes the dynamic of personality. Paul calls Christ "our life." In his Letter to the Philippians he said the same thing: ". . . life means Christ to me . . ." (Philippians 1:21, MOFFATT). In Galatians 2:20 he spoke of Christ living in him. Haven't we said, of a friend, "Music is his life," "Bridge is her life,"

"Sport is his life"? For the Christian, Christ, His love, and His way of dealing with persons and situations, are everything. He gives a man victory over lesser things, and delivers him from anxiety.

103

What the Resurrection Has Done for the World (*Sunday After Easter*)

BLESSED BE THE GOD AND FATHER OF OUR LORD JESUS CHRIST! BY HIS GREAT MERCY WE HAVE BEEN BORN ANEW TO A LIVING HOPE THROUGH THE RESURRECTION OF JESUS CHRIST FROM THE DEAD, AND TO AN INHERITANCE WHICH IS IMPERISHABLE, UNDEFILED, AND UNFADING, KEPT IN HEAVEN FOR YOU . . .—I PETER 1:3-4, RSV.

The first Sunday after Easter need not be "low Sunday" except in the liturgical calendar! It should be high in inspiration. Why not continue preaching the Good News of Christ's victory? The text sets the key and sounds the note of jubilant conviction. Why not ask, What is the "living hope" to which we have been "born anew"? What has Christ's resurrection done for the world? What has it meant for Jesus Himself? What may it mean to us?

I. It shows us that even when truth and goodness stand alone, these spiritual forces are stronger than all the physical powers arrayed against them. Had Jesus perished after His crucifixion we would never have known that evil could be defeated. Use George Bernard Shaw's *Saint Joan* as an illustration, particularly her speech to her tormentors, which begins: "Do not think you can frighten me by telling me that I am alone. France is alone; and God is alone." Who would you rather stand with, Joan or the men who burned her? With Paul or with Nero? With Jesus or with the religious authorities and government officials who condemned Him? Here James Russell Lowell's familiar words are relevant:

"Once to every man and nation comes the moment to decide. . . ."[7] Want to be on the winning side? Be on the right side. Which is the right side? Christ's side.

II. Love is more powerful than hate. Without the resurrection, would we have known that love never faileth? Hatred creates hatred; force arouses force; anger provokes anger. Look at human history. But when you refuse to hate, something new enters into the situation.

III. Christ's resurrection teaches that life is stronger than death when life is committed to the keeping and service of its Author and Redeemer. John 14:19 is true not only in a funeral chapel; it responds to every human need.

What did the resurrection mean for Jesus? Surely it meant liberation into life eternal and unlimited. Now He can operate everywhere. The resurrection vindicated every claim He made. He must have been all that He said He was; His teaching must have been true, for the universe responded to His claims, His trust and His love. Easter was the cosmic response and approval. What does the resurrection mean for us now that another Easter festival is over, and the triumphant strains of the anthems recede in memory? It means three things. (A) We need never walk alone, through any valley of shadow or on any height of danger, for the divine Contemporary is with us. (B) We can join the one team that must ultimately win against the forces of darkness, disease, superstition and war. (C) We will go through death to larger life. When bedtime comes, One whom we have learned to love and trust will say, "See you in the morning! More adventures tomorrow!"

104

Prepare for a Great Tomorrow
(*Sunday After Easter*)

> BEHOLD, I HAVE SET BEFORE YOU AN OPEN DOOR, WHICH
> NO ONE IS ABLE TO SHUT. . . . HOLD FAST WHAT YOU
> HAVE, SO THAT NO ONE MAY SEIZE YOUR CROWN—
> REVELATION 3:8, 11, RSV.

In the afterglow of Easter, Christians should know that the tomorrows will be great with meaning, possibility, life. But even Christians have their low Sundays and blue Mondays. As for secular man without the Biblical hope, he tries not to think too much about the future. Many adhere to the cynical view of Ecclesiastes: As things have been, so they will be; or, futility of futilities, all is futility. Forecasting continues to be popular, and we may be reasonably sure of certain things in the future: Not only death and taxes, but change (not always for the better); problems and tensions between individuals, races, power groups, nations; threats of war and planetary destruction; problems.

Whatever actually befalls us, the New Testament promises— for the believer in God through Jesus Christ, for the person who trusts and obeys the Lord of history and the Saviour of mankind— that tomorrow will be great. "Behold, I have set before you an open door. . . ." Here the preacher would be wise to recount the situation in the church in ancient Philadelphia to which John wrote this letter. The group was weak—"I know that you have little power . . ." (v. 8, RSV)—but it was steadfast in loyalty to God. The Christians in that city of brotherly love were urged to keep on keeping on. What does this letter say to us?

I. To believe hopefully in the future requires a well-nourished enthusiasm. Enthusiasm comes from Greek words *en theos*, meaning "in God." The "beat" character cannot hope, because he believes in nothing beyond his nerve ends and today.

II. Tomorrow will be great if we realize that God opens doors of opportunity for us today. We must not linger on the threshold or keep swinging on the gate marked "This way into service." Here the preacher might use the illustration of David Livingstone telling Cambridge University students that in Africa there was an open door. He told them to keep it open for Christianity and an abundant life. What about today, a century later? Africa, the giant, has awakened from a long sleep. Will she shut the door to Christian ideas, or only to imperialism that exploits her resources and people? What about the doors into Asia?

III. Let this assurance come with force to us as individuals: God opens a door of opportunity through a Christian vocation. Whether we are plumbers or preachers, artists or artisans, doctors or ditchdiggers, teachers or traders, we must glorify God through our calling, and witness to Christ in our job. What door are we using in this time of racial tension and nuclear war potential? What are we doing to enter, through Christ who is the Door, into communion with God Himself?

IV. Tomorrow will be great if we doubt our doubts about God's reality and His ultimate victory over opposing forces. Tomorrow will be great if we open our lives and the life of our church to the living Spirit who can make us pillars in the spiritual temple of the Most High. Do we believe that this is a planet visited by God Himself in the Son of His love, Jesus Christ? Do we believe that on the first Easter death died and the power of evil was broken? Do we live as men and women who believe that God maketh all things new, including tomorrow? Then we shall hold fast to our Lord and let no man rob us of the crown of victory.

105

God at Work (*Pentecost*)

SCRIPTURE LESSON—ACTS 2:1-13.

Pentecost was a supreme day for the Christian church. Whatever happened we may not know in detail, but if we study the subsequent history of the Christian enterprise we can never doubt that something happened. On that day the Holy Spirit came to the church in a tremendous way. While it is true that the eternal Spirit was active in revealing truth and God's will to men through all the ages, He came in new power and meaning at Pentecost. In a special way, God was at work.

I. The Holy Spirit was for those Christians the Source of all direction.

II. Leaders of the early church were Spirit-controlled and -empowered men.

III. Daily courage came to the disciples through the Spirit's invasion.

IV. This same power, direction, capacity to cope with life, and ability to win the world for Christ, can be ours.

Around the World in Sixty Minutes
(*World Communion*)

AND THIS GOSPEL OF THE KINGDOM WILL BE PREACHED
THROUGHOUT THE WHOLE WORLD . . .—MATTHEW 24:
14, RSV.

In a service of Christian worship we move, in imagination and concern, around the world within the hour usually devoted to our chief business as children of God. This is brought home to us vividly in the central service of Christian worship, the Lord's Supper.

I. At the Lord's table we are linked with persons of all races, cultures and nations who confess that Jesus Christ is Lord.

II. In praise and prayer we encompass humanity through our intercessions.

III. In worship we are united to participate in the world mission of the gospel.

IV. At the Lord's table we remember that while Christ died for us as individuals, he died for all, and we return to our homes and vocations as world citizens, inclusive and world-minded in our love.

Here, O Lord, We Offer (*World Communion*)

I APPEAL TO YOU THEREFORE, BRETHREN, BY THE MER-
CIES OF GOD, TO PRESENT YOUR BODIES AS A LIVING SAC-
RIFICE, HOLY AND ACCEPTABLE TO GOD, WHICH IS YOUR
SPIRITUAL WORSHIP—ROMANS 12:1, RSV.

At the heart of every Christian service of communion, whether it is called sacrament or ordinance, is the note of offering—first the sacrifice of God Himself in the Son of His love, and then our selves "as a living sacrifice, holy and acceptable to God." In every liturgy, this New Testament emphasis is proclaimed. Donald Soper has found in the structure of the communion service four acts of offering:[8]

I. The offering of our minds to God through the Word. Always the Word read and preached, however briefly, should precede the breaking, blessing, giving and receiving of the bread and the cup. Let us offer our minds to His mind and Spirit, that He may offer us His truth to make us free.

II. In the offertory we make a genuine offering of our material possessions. God, who has given us life, love, salvation and eternity, is the true Owner of everything that we possess. Primitive communism—all things in common—was soon and, I think, rightly, abandoned by the church. But it was never wholly forgotten that Christians must offer their material wealth to God for His use. We do this in our central act of worship by pooling our resources for the welfare of Christ's community. Dr. Soper declares, "The offertory in the sacrament of the Lord's Supper is the eternal declaration of the social gospel. . . . It is at one and the same time personal, spiritual, corporate, and economic." Under these symbols, do I offer my world of goods and possessions to God, and through Him to the Christian church? We could repeat the miracle of feeding the five thousand in country after country if we brought our resources to God that He might bless and use them.

III. We offer our thanksgiving to God for His unsurpassed gift of Christ. This indeed is the eucharistic or thanksgiving service of the whole church. To look at the cross is to be filled with "wonder, love and praise."[9]

IV. We offer ourselves to God, "no longer as sinners hoping for salvation, but as servants ready and equipped to do his will."

Dr. Soper has a concluding word for us:

Let a man make his offerings at the Holy Table, and I believe that he will be disposed thereby to believe in the reality of Christ's offer, and also, and best of all, that he will trust in his Lord to fulfill that offer in the common round and the daily task.

The Best Kind of Living (*Thanksgiving*)

YOU MAY BE THANKING GOD SPLENDIDLY, BUT IT
DOESN'T HELP THE OTHER MAN AT ALL—I CORINTHIANS
14:17, PHILLIPS.

I. Thanksgiving helps to make the best kind of living because an appreciative person is one who is glad for everything God gives.

II. Thanksgiving, not once a year but daily, makes for the best kind of living because each day brings something new to acknowledge with thanks.

III. Thanksgiving is the best kind of living because it places us in the best of company: the poets who wrote our psalms of praise, the companions of the Spirit who showed forth God's praise with their lips and in their lives, and Jesus who in His sacrament of love first gave thanks.

Miracle Medicine (*Thanksgiving*)

A CHEERFUL HEART IS A GOOD MEDICINE . . .—PRO-
VERBS 17:22, RSV.

John Henry Jowett said, "Gratitude is a vaccine, an antitoxin, and an antiseptic." What personality does not need such threefold protection against spiritual infection and soul-disease?

I. Let gratitude be a vaccine to prevent invasion by "germs" of bitterness, envy, "and all uncharitableness," as the prayer book has it. Albert Schweitzer cited reasons which led him to offer himself for the ministry of healing in Africa:

> It became steadily clearer to me that I had not the inward right to take as a matter of course my happy youth, my good health, and my power to work. Out of the depths of my feeling of happiness there grew up gradually within me an understanding of the saying of Jesus that we must not treat our lives as being for ourselves alone. Whoever is spared personal pain must feel himself called to help in diminishing the pain of others.[10]

"Count your blessings" is more than the refrain of an old gospel hymn. It is good therapy for a wounded spirit, and a vaccine that will keep out the viruses of discontent and disgruntlement.

II. Thanksgiving neutralizes the poisonous effects of fault-finding and complaining. Both Sir Walter Scott and Lord Byron were lame, but Scott was radiant, gallant and creative. However creative Byron may have been, he was known and remembered by many because he was embittered by his lameness. A difference in temperaments does not explain the difference in reactions to similar disabilities. Scott faced his handicap with Christian faith, grateful for the health and opportunities he had; Byron faced only his handicap.

An old woman, deprived of much that one would think necessary to a happy life, saw the ocean for the first time. She exclaimed, "I thank God for one thing of which there is enough!" Another person, looking for the first time at the Pacific Ocean, whined, "Well, there isn't as much of it as I expected!" Said John Ruskin, "The question is not what a man can scorn, disparage, or find fault with, but what he can love, value, and appreciate."

III. Gratitude is an antiseptic that purifies and soothes us when we are carrying burdens that chafe and fret our spirits. It is recorded of the Pilgrims in Plymouth that "at noon men staggered by reason of faintness for want of food, yet ere night, by the Good Providence and blessing of God, we have enjoyed such a plenty as though the windows of heaven had been opened to us." Harry C. Kennet said that Elder Brewster, sitting down to a meal of clams and a cup of cold water, looked up to heaven and returned thanks "for the abundance of the sea and for the treasures hid in the sand." In spite of their troubles and difficulties, the Pilgrims worked, prayed, and built homes in a new world—and they had their Thanksgiving Day.

Gratefully Yours (*Thanksgiving*)

> ...ALWAYS AND FOR EVERYTHING GIVING THANKS IN
> THE NAME OF OUR LORD JESUS CHRIST TO GOD THE
> FATHER—EPHESIANS 5:20, RSV.

How would you end a letter to God? "Lovingly"? "Hopefully"?
When you recall all you have received, for which no payment
could be made in money, services or things, "Gratefully yours"
would be in order. Certainly the New Testament makes clear that
a grateful attitude was one of the marks of the early Christian
church. Can we join this apostolic succession and come to God,
"Gratefully yours"?

I. Gratefully yours, O God, because Thy love has stooped to
save us. Recall the prayer of general thanksgiving: "For our creation, preservation, and all the blessings of this life; but above all
for the redemption of the world."

II. Gratefully yours, O God, because through Thy revelation
in the Bible, and supremely in Thy self-disclosure in Christ, we
know we cannot drift beyond Thy love and care.

III. Gratefully yours, for all things, because we cannot imagine
anything not from Thy mind and heart, nor can we believe that
anything in life cannot be used by Thee for a good purpose.

Notes

I CHRISTIAN LIVING

1. August, 1958, pp. 25-30.
2. Margaret Lane, *Biography of a Phenomenon* (Doubleday & Co., Inc.).
3. From the hymn by Charles Wesley.
4. From "On His Having Arrived At the Age of Twenty-three."
5. From "The Statue and the Bust."
6. Robert Louis Stevenson, "The Celestial Surgeon."
7. Abingdon Press, 1957, p. 350.
8. From "Peace," *Collected Poems,* p. 101. Copyright 1915 by Dodd, Mead and Company, Inc. Renewal copyright 1943 by Edward Marsh.
9. *Faithful Sayings* (The Epworth Press).
10. From the hymn "Love Divine, All Loves Excelling" by Charles Wesley.
11. From the hymn by Annie S. Hawks.

II CHRISTIAN CONVICTIONS

1. From *Christ and You.* Used by permission of the author.
2. Used by permission of Bishop Ensley.
3. Walter Chalmers Smith, *Olrig Grange.*
4. Abingdon Press, IX, 31-32.
5. From an article by Dr. William Barclay in *British Weekly,* London, England.
6. From the hymn by Cecil F. Alexander.
7. From the hymn "Sun of My Soul, Thou Saviour Dear" by John Keble.
8. *Ibid.*
9. From the hymn "Yield Not to Temptation" by Horatio R. Palmer.
10. W. Gordon Robinson, *New Testament Treasure,* Independent Press, Ltd.
11. *Ibid.*
12. *Time,* May 26, 1958.

13. Coventry Patmore.
14. *Eminent Victorians* (Harcourt, Brace and World, Inc.).
15. See *The Unutterable Beauty* by G. A. Studdert-Kennedy (Hodder & Stoughton, Ltd., 1930).
16. Henry Sloane Coffin, *Joy in Believing* (Charles Scribner's Sons).
17. Charles Wesley.
18. Washington Gladden.
19. From the hymn "God Is Love; His Mercy Brightens" by Sir John Bowring.
20. From the hymn "How Firm a Foundation, Ye Saints of the Lord," "K" in Rippon's *Selections.*
21. St. Ignatius of Antioch, *Epistle to the Smyrnaeans.*
22. *Daily Bible Readings,* published by The Committee on Publications, The Church of Scotland, Edinburgh, pp. 76-82.
23. From an article in *Think* magazine, published by Interna-
24. *Ibid.*
    tional Business Machines.
25. *New York Times,* April 27, 1958.
26. John Oxenham, "Credo," *Bees in Amber* (Fleming H. Revell Company, 1959), p. 16.

III CHRISTIAN ANTIDOTE FOR CRISIS

1. This famous declaration was made by the Protestant reformer, Theodore Beza. To the King of Navarre, who persecuted the Reformation church, Beza spoke the words the churches of France never forgot. " 'Sire,' he gravely said, 'it belongs in truth to the Church of God, in whose name I speak, to endure blows and not to inflict them. But it will also please your Majesty to remember that she is an anvil that has worn out many hammers.' " (From *Theodore Beza, the Counsellor of the French Revolution,* by Henry Martyn Baird. Published by G. P. Putnam's Sons.)
2. Jeanne Marie Bouvier de la Motte Guyon, 1767-91.
3. Boris Pasternak (Pantheon Books, Inc., 1958).

IV CHRISTIAN CALENDAR

1. *The Theology of the Sacraments* (Charles Scribner's Sons, 1957), p. 102.

2. *So Fight I.*
3. From the German, of *Angelus Silesius,* 1624-1677.
4. *The Life, the Question, and the Answer.*
5. *Out of My Life and Thought,* translated by C. T. Campion (Holt, Rinehart and Winston, Inc., 1949).
6. From an article in *The Presbyterian Outlook,* Richmond, Va.
7. From "The Present Crisis."
8. *All His Grace.* Outline used by permission of the author.
9. From the hymn "Love Divine, All Loves Excelling" by Charles Wesley.
10. *Op. cit.*

Index to Scriptures

OLD TESTAMENT

NEW TESTAMENT

APOCRYPHA

Index